The Politics of Policy Analysis

Paul Cairney

The Politics of Policy Analysis

palgrave
macmillan

Paul Cairney
Division of History, Heritage, and Politics
University of Stirling
Stirling, UK

ISBN 978-3-030-66121-2   ISBN 978-3-030-66122-9 (eBook)
https://doi.org/10.1007/978-3-030-66122-9

© The Editor(s) (if applicable) and The Author(s), under exclusive licence to Springer Nature Switzerland AG 2021
This work is subject to copyright. All rights are solely and exclusively licensed by the Publisher, whether the whole or part of the material is concerned, specifically the rights of translation, reprinting, reuse of illustrations, recitation, broadcasting, reproduction on microfilms or in any other physical way, and transmission or information storage and retrieval, electronic adaptation, computer software, or by similar or dissimilar methodology now known or hereafter developed.
The use of general descriptive names, registered names, trademarks, service marks, etc. in this publication does not imply, even in the absence of a specific statement, that such names are exempt from the relevant protective laws and regulations and therefore free for general use.
The publisher, the authors and the editors are safe to assume that the advice and information in this book are believed to be true and accurate at the date of publication. Neither the publisher nor the authors or the editors give a warranty, expressed or implied, with respect to the material contained herein or for any errors or omissions that may have been made. The publisher remains neutral with regard to jurisdictional claims in published maps and institutional affiliations.

Cover pattern © Melisa Hasan

This Palgrave Macmillan imprint is published by the registered company Springer Nature Switzerland AG.
The registered company address is: Gewerbestrasse 11, 6330 Cham, Switzerland

Preface: Combining Insights on Policymaking and Policy Analysis

New texts in policy analysis suggest that they are describing something new. Studies *of policy analysts* suggest that their number, role, and status have changed profoundly over several decades. New texts on *how to do* policy analysis reflect those changes somewhat. However, many still focus on the idea that the primary role of analysts is to communicate a simple message about a complex problem, for a powerful client with the power to act on their recommendations.

This book identifies two key ways to improve the literature. First, explore the implications of new developments in policy process research, on the role of psychology in communication, and the multi-centric nature of policymaking. Second, incorporate insights from studies of power, co-production, feminism, and decolonisation, to redraw the boundaries of policy-relevant knowledge. These insights help raise new questions and change expectations about the role and impact of policy analysis.

In other words, let's improve policy analysis by combining insights from many approaches. If done well, it fosters a language that people from different disciplines and professions can use to communicate. I used this approach in *The Politics of Evidence-Based Policymaking* (Cairney 2016). I was trying to help researchers in disciplines such as public health and climate change studies to engage with theories of policymaking. If successful, learning can be mutual. Policy studies help researchers understand how their evidence fits into the bigger picture, and why they should not expect policymaking to be 'evidence-based'. Health, environmental, and social researchers help policy scholars understand key interdisciplinary concerns. For example, many ask 'why don't policymakers listen to my evidence?' and I try to answer this question in most guest talks (e.g. Cairney 2018). However, it did not occur to me until reading work by Oliver et al. (2014) that called for more policy theory insights in this field.

In *this* book, the conversation is between researchers of policy analysis, policy processes, and critical accounts that identify the role of power, inequalities, marginalisation, racism, or colonisation on the use of research in policy. In this conversation, there is a more established crossover between approaches (and a field called 'critical policy analysis'). Policy analysis texts give advice on how to write reports for clients with reference to power and a political context to which analysts must adapt. Many writers have experience in politics as analysts or other actors, and their advice on being pragmatic or concise reflects their experience of that environment. However, I suggest that these accounts do not go far enough, in two main ways.

First, they see this world through the eyes of individual analysts or clients. In contrast, policy process research is about policymaking systems containing large numbers of political actors. To 'zoom out' is to see policy analysis as part of a bigger picture over which individuals have limited knowledge and even less control. This big picture has profound implications for the overall role and impact of analysis. Second, they give insufficient attention to power and inequalities in politics. Critical studies identify the ways in which some groups are marginalised, from researchers dismissing their claims to knowledge to policymakers adopting 'solutions' that cause a disproportionately negative impact on their lives.

In that context, a conversation between each approach helps highlight key issues in policy analysis and prompt reflection on how to respond. In Part I, I summarise key texts in each field and ask how policy analysis advice reflects wider concerns. In Part II, I explore key themes to which each field may contribute. This book consists of a large number of short thematic sections (2–5000 words). I developed each theme via a series of blog posts, which review policy analysis texts and connect their insights to wider political and policymaking themes: *Policy Analysis in 750 Words* (https://paulcairney.wordpress.com/policy-analysis-in-750-words/). This series (a) summarises key texts, (b) relates them to each other and to key themes, and (c) provides scope for more posts, to produce a project that keeps talking even after you close the book. The benefit of this book-and-blog format is as follows.

PREFACE: COMBINING INSIGHTS ON POLICYMAKING AND POLICY ANALYSIS   vii

1. *An introduction to the existing field*
   - The posts summarise each policy analysis text, which you can use as: a companion to further reading, and a way to compare texts without reading every book on the market.
   - The book brings together a discussion of this field as a whole, to identify its common elements and explore the benefits and drawbacks to five-step policy analysis. It encourages reflection on the field of mainstream policy analysis to help imagine new forms of analysis that are as practical but also more inclusive of multiple perspectives.
2. *A connection between policy analysis and policy process texts*
   - The posts introduce themes that connect policy analysis to policy process research, in an accessible way (supplemented by the 500- and 1000-word posts and *Understanding Public Policy*—Cairney 2020). Both are crucial to our understanding of policymaking.
   - This book discusses how policy theories shape our overall understanding of policy analysis. Frankly, without applying this contextual knowledge, a policy analyst would produce recommendations untethered from policymaking reality.
3. *An introduction to critical policy analysis*
   - The posts provide a flavour of a much wider literature that should inform mainstream policy analysis. Some texts engage directly with policy analysis texts. However, many more studies are relevant even if the connections do not seem clear at first.
4. This book connects mainstream and critical policy analysis, and wider critical social science texts, to imagine a form of policy analysis that highlights social and economic inequalities and sees policy analysis as a way to foster equity and human dignity.

Overall, the blog introduces the field and the book synthesises its insights to imagine a different future. I will add further summaries of key texts (and record short podcasts) to treat the project as akin to a 'living document' that updates continuously. In contrast to Cairney (2016), I try not to 'synthesise' their insights *too much* to tell my story of policy analysis. Instead, you will find relatively extensive summaries of exemplars in the fields of policy analysis and more critical approaches to politics and policy analysis. However, it remains my story of the work of other people, which is no substitute for the real thing (particularly since I only scratch the surface of texts on critical social science). So, please treat this discussion as a way into new studies, not an attempt to give the final word.

Stirling, UK   Paul Cairney

References

Cairney, P. (2016). *The Politics of Evidence-Based Policymaking*. London: Palgrave Pivot.

Cairney, P. (2018, October 11). The Politics of Evidence-Based Policymaking: ANZSOG Talks. *Paul Cairney: Politics & Public Policy*. Retrieved from https://paulcairney.wordpress.com/2018/10/11/the-politics-of-evidence-based-policymaking-anzsog-talks/.

Cairney, P. (2019). Policy Analysis in 750 Words. *Paul Cairney: Politics & Public Policy*. Retrieved from https://paulcairney.wordpress.com/policy-analysis-in-750-words/.

Oliver, K., Lorenc, T., & Innvar, S. (2014b). New Directions in Evidence-Based Policy Research: A Critical Analysis of the Literature. *Health Research Policy and Systems, 12* (34), 1–11. Retrieved from http://www.biomedcentral.com/content/pdf/1478-4505-12-34.pdf.

Contents

Part I	State of the Art Policy Analysis Texts	1
1	Introduction: New Policy Analysis for the Real World	3
2	What Is the Classic Five-Step Model of *How to Do* Policy Analysis?	11
3	What Has Changed, and Why Do We Need New Policy Analysis?	33
4	What Insights from Policy Process Research Do Policy Analysts Need to Know?	49
5	What Insights from Wider Studies of Power, Knowledge, Politics, and Policy Do Policy Analysts Need to Consider?	71
6	How Have *How to Do* Policy Analysis Texts Incorporated These Insights So Far?	91
Part II	Challenging Themes in Policy Analysis	97
7	Comparing What You Need as a Policy Analyst with Policymaking Reality	99

8	Who Should Be Involved in the Process of Policy Analysis?	109
9	What Is Your Role as a Policy Analyst?	117
10	How to Be a Policy Entrepreneur	123
11	Policy Analysis as Systems Thinking	129
12	How Much Impact Can You Expect from Your Analysis?	139
13	Conclusion: Combining Insights on Policy Analysis	147

Annex: What Do We Want Public Policy Scholars to Learn?		153
Index		167

List of Figures

Fig. 4.1   The policy cycle versus infinite cycles. (Source: Cairney 2017)   55
Fig. 4.2   An image of the policy process. (Source: Cairney 2017)   55
Fig. 4.3   The ACF flow diagram. (Source: Weible et al. 2016: 6)   62

LIST OF TABLES

Table 3.1	Policy analysis in the 'rational' and real world	35
Table 8.1	Two stories of knowledge-informed policy analysis	112
Table 11.1	Ten stories of systems thinking	130
Table 13.1	Three perspectives on five-step policy analysis methods	150
Table A1	Key topics and question in basic and applied policy sciences	155

List of Boxes

Box 2.1	Bardach (2012) and Bardach and Patashnik (2020) A Practical Guide for Policy Analysis	12
Box 2.2	Dunn (2017) Public Policy Analysis	13
Box 2.3	Meltzer and Schwartz (2019) Policy Analysis as Problem-Solving	13
Box 2.4	Mintrom (2012) Contemporary Policy Analysis	14
Box 2.5	Weimer and Vining (2017) Policy Analysis: Concepts and Practice	14
Box A1	Rationale for Three-Minute Presentation	158
Box A2	Rationale for Policy Analysis and Reflection	161
Box A3	Rationale for Blog Post 1	163
Box A4	Rationale for the Essay	165
Box A5	Rationale for Blog Post 2	165

PART I

State of the Art Policy Analysis Texts

Part I presents a discussion of policy analysis texts. It identifies how they connect to studies of policy analysts, policy processes, and critical accounts of social science and policy analysis. It then asks how they incorporate these insights and what more they could do.

CHAPTER 1

Introduction: New Policy Analysis for the Real World

Abstract New studies of policy analysts suggest that the old ways of doing policy analysis are gone. Modern 'how to do policy analysis' texts reflect this novelty somewhat, but not enough. One cause of the problem is a too-wide gap between policy analysis and policy process research. The other cause is insufficient attention to the politics of knowledge use. We should use insights from each field to close that gap.

Keywords Policy analysis • Policy process research • Policy studies • Critical policy analysis

INTRODUCTION

Policy analysis is the identification of a policy problem and possible solutions. Some analyses stop at that point, while others monitor and evaluate outcomes. There are many classic guides to help budding policy analysts produce the research necessary to define problems and evaluate potential solutions, and to communicate their findings, in a political context. Many classic texts focus on analytical tools such as cost-benefit analysis, but most are informed by political science and the idea that policy analysis is more 'art and craft' (Wildavsky 1980) than a method or science. They emphasise the requirement of a policy solution's technical *and* political feasibility. A solution should work as intended if implemented *and* be important and acceptable to enough powerful actors in a policymaking system. This focus on pragmatism extends to communication, in which the tradition is to turn a profoundly complex issue into a simple executive summary. Similarly, evaluations of policy solutions involve research methods and a technical language to produce findings, and there is a literature devoted to how people communicate those findings more-or-less effectively to make an impact on policy (Weiss 1977, 1979).

However, new texts in policy analysis suggest that they are describing something new. Studies *of policy analysts* suggest that their number, role, set of required skills, and status have changed profoundly over several decades. There are many styles of policy analysis from which to choose, to address (a) the different contexts in which analysts engage and (b) the highly political ways in which analysts generate policy-relevant knowledge.

Texts on *how to do* policy analysis reflect those changes *somewhat*, and most texts describe the relationship between analysis and political environment. However, many texts also hold on to the idea that the primary role of analysts is to communicate a simple message about a complex problem, for a powerful client with the power to act on their recommendations. They focus primarily on the *mechanics* of policy analysis, *from the perspective of the potential analyst*, rather than the wider politics of policy analysis and the complexity of the policymaking system in which they engage.

One cause of this problem is the often-wide gap between two aspects of the 'policy sciences' described by Lasswell (1951, 1956, 1971):

1. Policy process research: the analysis *of* policy or knowledge *of* the policy process.
2. Policy analysis: analysis *for* policy or knowledge *in* the process.

Lasswell's original idea was that both elements are analytically separable but mutually informative: policy analysis is crucial to solving real policy problems (to advance 'human dignity'), policy process research informs the feasibility of analysis, and the study of policy analysts informs research. His original vision was to use policy process research to identify the policymaking context and the tools of policy analysis to provide a systematic way to think about how to identify and solve problems within it.

Yet, Cairney and Weible (2017) argue that these two separate concerns—to describe policymaking and prescribe action—have diverged. Policy process research has morphed into a 'basic science' in which the audience of policy theorists is primarily a group of other policy theorists.

There is clear potential to translate their insights to a wider audience, and there are many notable attempts to do it systematically (Weible et al. 2012; Shipan and Volden 2012; Cairney 2015, 2016; Cairney et al. 2019; Weible and Cairney 2018). However, there is a stronger professional incentive to focus on theory development and empirical research and to publish it for a small audience in high-profile political science journals.

The unintended consequence is a highly specialised field of policy theory in which there are barriers to entry: it takes a lot of time and effort to decode the policy theory jargon, understand each theory or approach in depth, and understand how the insights of one theory relate to another (Cairney 2013). There are blogs and textbooks designed for this task, but they either scratch the surface of the field (Cairney 2020; John 2012), provide a huge amount of material (Parsons 1995), or summarise theories without decoding them enough to make them accessible to new readers (Weible and Sabatier 2018). There is no substitute for intense and sustained study to understand this field in sufficient depth and relate it to wider insights in social science, but most policy analysts do not have the time or incentive to learn so intensively from this field. The 'opportunity cost' is high. Instead of reading a jargon-filled literature, with no clear and direct payoff to policy analysis, students can go straight to the relatively clear and simple tools of policy analysis. The latter give them step-by-step guides to policy analysis which incorporate *some* political and policy research insights, but with a far greater emphasis on methods such as cost-benefit analysis than topics such as power, policymaker psychology, complexity, or policy change (Weimer and Vining 2017). If so, budding policy analysts would benefit from engagement with a synthesised version of the wider literature—including studies of policy processes and the politics of knowledge production—to reflect more widely on their role and their task.

Therefore, this book identifies two ways to expand the policy analysis literature in a manageable way. *First*, explore the implications of new developments in policy process research, on the role of psychology in communication and the multi-centric nature of policymaking. Policy analysts engage with policymakers who engage emotionally with information and operate in an environment over which they have limited understanding and even less control. One factor requires analysts to consider how far they should go to persuade policymakers with analysis, and the other should make them wonder how much power their audience has to influence policy outcomes. *Second*, incorporate insights from studies of power, co-production, feminism, racism, and decolonisation, to redraw the boundaries of policy process research and interrogate the status of policy-relevant knowledge. In particular, describing policy analysis as a largely technical process, using five-step analyses to serve clients, is itself an exercise of power to downplay the politics of knowledge production and use. The alternative is to reflect on whose policy-relevant knowledge counts, and should count.

These insights may not change classic recommendations on the practice of policy analysis, since analysts still need simple heuristics to guide their work. However, they change profoundly the expectations that analysts should have about their role and impact on policy and policymaking. Readers may still end up recommending and using five-step policy analysis models, but also question what they are for, and how to think about the wider political context associated with each step. At the very least, this wider reflection helps policy analysts remain adept at responding to the many different contexts they will face when they do their work.

Structure of the Book

This book presents a series of sections on what we know so far about policy analysis, what we gain from a wider examination of the politics of policy analysis in a complex policymaking environment, and the unanswered questions that emerge from this approach. The first half presents some contextual questions to highlight new developments in the fields of policy analysis and policy process research:

1. What is the classic five-step model of *how to do* policy analysis?
2. What has changed, and why do we need new policy analysis?
3. What insights from policy process research do policy analysts need to know?
4. What insights from wider studies of power, knowledge, politics, and policy do policy analysts need to consider?
5. How have *how to do* policy analysis texts incorporated these insights so far?

This coverage of well-established policy analysis texts, studies of the policy process, and wider debates and research on the politics of knowledge allows us to explore a series of themes on how to reconsider common policy analysis advice. The second half addresses the following questions or themes.

1. *Comparing what you need as a policy analyst with policymaking reality.*

Five-step guides relate more to the functional requirements of policy analysis than real-world policymaking. Policy concepts and theories tell us that 'bounded rationality' limits the comprehensiveness of policy analysis, and complexity undermines policymakers' understanding and engagement in policy processes. Policy analysis takes place in a policymaking environment over which no one has full knowledge or control. There is no all-powerful 'centre' able to control policy outcomes via a series of steps in a policy cycle. Therefore, who is your audience when you define problems, and what can you realistically expect them to do with your solutions?

2. *Who should be involved in the process of policy analysis?*

Policy analysis is a political act to decide who should be involved in the policy process. There are competing visions of analysis, from a focus on 'evidence-based' policymaking built on a small group of experts, to a 'co-produced' exercise built on deliberation and wide inclusion.

3. *What is your role as a policy analyst?*

Reflections on policy analysis should include: who should decide how to frame and solve policy problems, how pragmatic should you be when proposing policy change, and to what extent is your policy success dependent on processes to generate inclusion, as opposed simply to a focus on outcomes. This section identifies a series of policy analyst archetypes, but argues that most can be grouped into two main approaches: (1) the pragmatic or professional, client-oriented policy analyst and (2) the questioning, storytelling, or decolonising policy analyst.

4. *How to be a policy entrepreneur?*

Mintrom highlights the role of policy entrepreneurship in policy analysis, focusing on attributes, skills, and strategies for effective analysis. However, policy studies suggest that most policy actors such as entrepreneurs fail, their environments better explain their success, and relatively few people are in the position to become entrepreneurs.

5. *Policy analysis as systems thinking.*

The idea of 'systems thinking' is potentially useful to policy analysis, but only if we can clarify its meaning. This section highlights ten different meanings, which can be reduced to two contradictory findings: policy analysts and policymakers can exercise power to have a *maximal* or *minimal* effect on policy. The latter suggests that systems thinking is about how to adapt to a system out of your control.

6. *How much impact can you expect from your analysis? How far would you go to secure it?*

This section identifies the policy analysis strategies associated with maximising impact, subject to a context that can help maximise or minimise policymaker interest. It then asks how far analysts should go to get what they want from their engagement with policymakers. I introduce a 'ladder of ethical engagement' to use policy theory insights to inform policy analysis strategy.

In each case, the overall theme relates to a renewed focus on the policy sciences: what can the study of policy analysis tell us about policymaking, and what can studies of policymaking tell budding policy analysts about the nature of their task in relation to their policymaking environment? What is the ethical approach to policy analysis and the pursuit of 'human dignity', given the high levels of inequalities and marginalisation in political systems?

References

Cairney, P. (2013). Standing on the Shoulders of Giants: How Do We Combine the Insights of Multiple Theories in Public Policy Studies? *Policy Studies Journal*, *41*(1), 1–21.

Cairney, P. (2015). How Can Policy Theory Have an Impact on Policy Making?' *Teaching. Public Administration*, *33*(1), 22–39.

Cairney, P. (2016). *The Politics of Evidence-based Policymaking*. London: Palgrave Pivot.

Cairney, P. (2020). *Understanding Public Policy* (2nd ed.). London: Red Globe.

Cairney, P., Heikkila, T., & Wood, M. (2019). *Making Policy in a Complex World*. Cambridge: Cambridge University Press.

Cairney, P., & Weible, C. (2017). The New Policy Sciences: Combining The Cognitive Science of Choice, Multiple Theories of Context, and Basic and Applied Analysis. *Policy Sciences*, *50*(4), 619–627.

John, P. (2012). *Analysing Public Policy* (2nd ed.). London: Routledge.

Lasswell, H. (1956). *The Decision Process: Seven Categories of Functional Analysis*. College Park, MD: University of Maryland Press.

Lasswell, H. (1971). *A Pre-view of the Policy Sciences*. New York: American Elsevier Publishing.

Lasswell, H. D. (1951). The Policy Orientation. In D. Lerner & H. Lasswell (Eds.), *The Policy Sciences*. Stanford, CA: Stanford University Press.

Parsons, W. (1995). *Public Policy*. Aldershot: Edward Elgar.

Shipan, C., & Volden, C. (2012). Policy Diffusion: Seven Lessons for Scholars and Practitioners. *Public Administration Review, 72*(6), 788–796.

Weible, C., & Cairney, P. (2018). Practical Lessons from Theories. *Policy and Politics, 46*(2), 183–197.

Weible, C., Heikkila, T., deLeon, P., & Sabatier, P. (2012). Understanding and Influencing the Policy Process. *Policy Sciences, 45*(1), 1–21.

Weible, C., & Sabatier, P. (2018). *Theories of the Policy Process* (4th ed.). Chicago: Westview Press.

Weimer, D., & Vining, A. (2017). *Policy Analysis: Concepts and Practice* (6th ed.). London: Routledge.

Weiss, C. (1977). *Using Social Research in Public Policy-Making*. Lexington: D. C. Heath.

Weiss, C. (1979). The Many Meanings of Research Utilization. *Public Administration Review, 39*(5), 426–431.

Wildavsky, A. (1980). *The Art and Craft of Policy Analysis*. London: Macmillan.

CHAPTER 2

What Is the Classic Five-Step Model of *How to Do* Policy Analysis?

Abstract This chapter summarises insights from many classic policy analysis texts. Most are client-oriented, describing key steps, including define a policy problem identified by your client; identify technically and politically feasible solutions; use value-based criteria and political goals to compare solutions; predict the outcome of each feasible solution; and make a recommendation to your client.

Keywords Policy analysis • Problem definition • Policy solutions • Cost-benefit analysis • Forecasting

INTRODUCTION

Classic models of policy analysis are client-oriented. Most 'how to' guides are *ex ante* (before the event), focused primarily on defining a problem, and predicting the effect of solutions, to inform a client's current choice. Few, such as Dunn (2017), also emphasise *ex post* (after the event) policy analysis, to include monitoring and evaluating that choice. Most texts identify the steps that a policy analysis should follow, from identifying a problem and potential solutions to finding ways to predict and evaluate the impact of each solution. Each text describes this process in different ways, as outlined in Boxes 2.1, 2.2, 2.3, 2.4, and 2.5 (with the exception of Dunn, the italicized advice in boxed text is verbatim). However, for the most part, they follow the same five steps:

© The Author(s), under exclusive license to Springer Nature Switzerland AG 2021
P. Cairney, *The Politics of Policy Analysis*,
https://doi.org/10.1007/978-3-030-66122-9_2

> **Box 2.1 Bardach (2012) and Bardach and Patashnik (2020) A Practical Guide for Policy Analysis**
>
> 1. *Define the problem.* Provide a diagnosis of a policy problem, using rhetoric and eye-catching data to generate attention.
> 2. *Assemble some evidence.* Gather relevant data efficiently.
> 3. *Construct the alternatives.* Identify the relevant and feasible policy solutions that your audience might consider.
> 4. *Select the criteria.* Typical value judgements relate to efficiency, equity, and fairness, the trade-off between individual freedom and collective action, and the extent to which a policy process involves citizens in deliberation.
> 5. *Project the outcomes.* Focus on the outcomes that key actors care about (such as value for money), and quantify and visualise your predictions if possible.
> 6. *Confront the trade-offs.* Compare the pros and cons of each solution, such as how much of a bad service policymakers will accept to cut costs.
> 7. *Decide.* Examine your case through the eyes of a policymaker.
> 8. *Tell your story.* Identify your target audience and tailor your case. Weigh up the benefits of oral versus written presentation. Provide an executive summary. Focus on coherence and clarity. Keep it simple and concise. Avoid jargon.
>
> Note: With the exception of Dunn, the italicised advice is verbatim.

1. Define a policy problem identified by your client.
2. Identify technically and politically feasible solutions.
3. Use value-based criteria and political goals to compare solutions.
4. Predict the outcome of each feasible solution.
5. Make a recommendation to your client.

Further, they share the sense that analysts need to adapt pragmatically to a political environment. Assume that your audience is not an experienced policy analyst. Assume a political environment in which there is limited attention or time to consider problems, and some

Box 2.2   Dunn (2017) Public Policy Analysis

1. *What is the policy problem to be solved?* Identify its severity, urgency, cause, and our ability to solve it. Don't define the wrong problem, such as by oversimplifying.
2. *What effect will each potential policy solution have?* 'Forecasting' methods can help provide 'plausible' predictions about the future effects of current/alternative policies.
3. *Which solutions should we choose, and why?* Normative assessments are based on values, such as 'equality, efficiency, security, democracy, enlightenment', and beliefs about the preferable balance between state, communal, and market/individual solutions (2017: 6; 205).
4. *What were the policy outcomes?* 'Monitoring' is crucial because it is difficult to predict policy success, and unintended consequences are inevitable (2017: 250).
5. *Did the policy solution work as intended? Did it improve policy outcomes?* Try to measure the outcomes of your solution, while noting that evaluations are contested (2017: 332–41).

Box 2.3   Meltzer and Schwartz (2019) Policy Analysis as Problem-Solving

1. *Define the problem.* Problem definition is a political act of framing, as part of a narrative to evaluate the nature, cause, size, and urgency of an issue.
2. *Identify potential policy options (alternatives) to address the problem.* Identify many possible solutions, then select the 'most promising' for further analysis (2019: 65).
3. *Specify the objectives to be attained in addressing the problem and the criteria to evaluate the attainment of these objectives as well as the satisfaction of other key considerations (e.g., equity, cost, equity, feasibility).*
4. *Assess the outcomes of the policy options in light of the criteria and weigh trade-offs between the advantages and disadvantages of the options.*
5. *Arrive at a recommendation.* Make a preliminary recommendation to inform an iterative process, drawing feedback from clients and stakeholder groups (2019: 212).

Note: Meltzer and Schwartz (2019: 22–3) also provide a table of 'quite similar' steps described by Bardach and Patashnik, Patton et al., Stokey and Zeckhauser, Hammond et al., and Weimer and Vining.

Box 2.4 Mintrom (2012) Contemporary Policy Analysis

1. *Engage in problem definition.* Define the nature of a policy problem, and the role of government in solving it, while engaging with many stakeholders (2012: 3; 58–60).
2. *Propose alternative responses to the problem.* Identify how governments have addressed comparable problems, and a previous policy's impact (2012: 21).
3. *Choose criteria for evaluating each alternative policy response.* 'Effectiveness, efficiency, fairness, and administrative efficiency' are common (2012: 21).
4. *Project the outcomes of pursuing each policy alternative.* Estimate the cost of a new policy, in comparison with current policy, and in relation to factors such as savings to society or benefits to certain populations.
5. *Identify and analyse trade-offs among alternatives.* Use your criteria and projections to compare each alternative in relation to their likely costs and benefits.
6. *Report findings and make an argument for the most appropriate response.* Client-oriented advisors identify the beliefs of policymakers and tailor accordingly (2012: 22).

Box 2.5 Weimer and Vining (2017) Policy Analysis: Concepts and Practice

1. *Write to Your Client.* Having a client such as an elected policymaker requires you to address the question they ask, by their deadline, in a clear and concise way that they can understand (and communicate to others) quickly (2017: 23; 370–4).
2. *Understand the Policy Problem.* First, 'diagnose the undesirable condition'. Second, frame it as 'a market or government failure (or maybe both)'.

(*continued*)

Box 2.5 (continued)

3. *Be Explicit About Values (and goals)*. Identify (a) the values to prioritise, such as 'efficiency', 'equity', and 'human dignity', and (b) 'instrumental goals', such as 'sustainable public finance or political feasibility', to generate support for solutions.
4. *Specify Concrete Policy Alternatives*. Explain potential solutions in sufficient detail to predict the costs and benefits of each 'alternative' (including current policy).
5. *Predict and Value Impacts*. Short deadlines dictate that you use 'logic and theory, rather than systematic empirical evidence' to make predictions efficiently (2017: 27).
6. *Consider the Trade-Offs*. Each alternative will fulfil certain goals more than others. Produce a summary table to make value-based choices about trade-offs (2017: 356–8).
7. *Make a Recommendation*. 'Unless your client asks you not to do so, you should explicitly recommend one policy' (2017: 28).

policy solutions will be politically infeasible. Describe the policy problem for your audience: to help them see it as something worthy of their energy. Discuss a small number of possible solutions, the differences between them, and their respective costs and benefits. Keep it short with the aid of visual techniques that sum up the issue concisely, to minimise cognitive load and make the problem seem solvable (Cairney and Kwiatkowski 2017).

Further, each of the approaches in Boxes 2.1, 2.2, 2.3, 2.4, and 2.5 describes the same core themes guiding the analysis. The core themes are described below.

Most Policy Analysis Is Client-Oriented

Having a client such as an elected policymaker, or governmental or non-governmental organisation, requires you to tailor your analysis to their needs, including:

1. *Meet their deadline, and be concise.* Address the question they ask, by their chosen deadline, in a clear and concise way, that they can understand and communicate to others quickly (Weimer and Vining 2017: 23; 370–4).
2. *See problems and solutions through their eyes.* Speak with the consumers of your evidence to anticipate their reaction (Bardach 2012). Find out how they seek to use your analysis, and their ability to make or influence the policies you might suggest (Meltzer and Schwartz 2019: 49). Questions to your client may include: what is your organisation's 'mission', what is feasible in terms of resources and politics, which stakeholders do you want to include, and how will you define success (2019: 105–12)?
3. *Identify their beliefs.* Anticipate the policy options worth researching, albeit while not simply telling clients what they want to hear (Mintrom 2012: 22).

Only some discussions highlight the wider value of analysis. For example, Weimer and Vining (2017) emphasise the benefit of showing your work, to emphasise the general value of policy analysis, and anticipate a change in circumstances or the choice by your client to draw different conclusions. Further, Mintrom (2012: 5) discusses the possibility that analysts, 'who want to change the world', research options that are often not politically feasible in the short term but are too important to ignore (such as gender mainstreaming or action to address climate change).

Problem Definition Has a Technical Element, But Is Always About Power and Politics

To some extent, problem definition is a technical exercise conducted with limited resources and in cooperation with others. Problem definition requires analysts to gather sufficient data on its severity, urgency, cause, and our ability to solve it (Dunn 2017). Recognise that you are not an expert in the policy problem, but don't define the wrong problem by generating insufficient knowledge (Weimer and Vining 2017). Recognise the value of multiple perspectives, such as from many stakeholders with different views (Dunn 2017; Meltzer and Schwartz 2019: 40–5; Mintrom 2012: 3; 58–60).

This process may *begin* from a client's perspective, but avoid defining a problem so narrowly that it closes off discussion too quickly (Meltzer and Schwartz 2019: 51–2). Place your client's initial 'diagnosis' in a wider perspective (Weimer and Vining 2017). Define the nature and size of a policy problem, and *the role of government in solving it* (Mintrom 2012). Then, frame it as 'a market or government failure (or maybe both)', to show how individual or collective choices produce inefficient allocations of resources and poor outcomes (Weimer and Vining 2017: 59–201).

As such, problem definition is a juggling act, containing data, client perspectives, and a professional commitment to a wider view. As Mintrom describes, engage with your audience to work out what they need and when, use your 'critical abilities' to ask yourself 'why they have been presented in specific ways, what their sources might be, and why they have arisen at this time', and present 'alternative scenarios' (2012: 22; 20; 27; 81). Meltzer and Schwarz prompt you to ask yourself if you can generate a timeline, identify key stakeholders, and place a 'boundary' on the problem. Establish if the problem is urgent, who cares about it, and who else might care (2019: 46). 'Map' causation with reference to individual and structural causes, intended and unintended consequences, simple and complex causation, market or government failure, and/or the ability to blame an individual or organisation (2019: 48–9). Combine quantitative and qualitative data to frame problems in relation to severity, trends in severity, novelty, proximity to your audience, and urgency or crisis (2019: 53–4). For Dunn (2017), 'problem-structuring methods' are crucial, to: compare ways to define or interpret a problem and ward against making too many assumptions about its nature and cause; produce models of cause-and-effect; and make a problem seem solvable, such as by placing boundaries on its coverage. These methods foster creativity, which is useful when issues seem new and ambiguous, or new solutions are in demand (2017: 54; 69; 77; 81–107).

However, problem definition is primarily a political process involving actors exercising power—through argumentation—to make sure that policymakers see a problem from a particular perspective (2017: 79). Policy analysts are not objective observers of this process. Rather, their analysis is part of a narrative to evaluate the nature, cause, size, and urgency of an issue (Meltzer and Schwartz 2019: 38–40). As such, analysts need to find effective ways to be influential in that context (Bardach 2012). They also need to reflect on their own biases, and those of their clients, and how they might negotiate problem definition in that context (Meltzer and Schwartz 2019: 37–8; 50; 279–82). This political process extends to the evaluation of policies, since few problems are solved, and debates on the success or failure of previous initiatives often set the current agenda (Dunn 2017: 57). If so, recognise whose evaluations or interests seem to count in such debates. Put most starkly, facts about the impacts of policy on people have little meaning until we decide whose experiences matter, and our values and beliefs influence how we gauge success (Dunn 2017: 322–32).

Policy Instruments Can Be Technically Feasible But Politically Infeasible (or Vice Versa)

Bardach's (2012) classic advice is to assess a potential policy solution's technical *and* political feasibility. Some solutions may appear to be technically effective but too unpopular. Therefore, identify the relevant and feasible policy solutions that your audience *might consider*, preferably by identifying how the solution would work if implemented as intended. Think of solutions as on a spectrum of acceptability, according to the extent to which your audience will accept (say) market or state action. Then, establish a baseline to help measure the impact of marginal policy changes, and compare costs and benefits in relation to something tangible (such as money). Your list can include things governments already do (such as tax or legislate), or a new policy design. Focus on the extent to which you are locking-in policymakers to your solution even if it proves to be ineffective (if you need to invest in new capital) (Bardach 2012).

In other words, political feasibility can relate strongly to the status quo and extent to which a new policy looks like it represents major change. In that context, Mintrom recommends trying to generate knowledge about how governments have addressed comparable problems in the past or in relation to another problem, and identifying the cause of that policy's impact and if it would have the same effect in this case (2012: 211; 76–7). In doing so, consider the wider *political context*, to anticipate how policymakers, implementers, target populations, and publics would react, and *policymaking context*, in which policies and institutions already exist to address most policy problems in some way (2012: 20).

While Meltzer and Schwartz (2019: 65–9) incorporate such strategies, they also note the new development of policy instruments derived from the study of psychology and behavioural public policy (2019: 79–90; John 2018). More importantly, they focus on the role of 'design thinking' to help identify—at least initially—a wider range of possible solutions. In doing so, learn from design principles—including 'empathy', 'co-creating' policy with service users or people affected, and 'prototyping'—and compare alternatives in 'good faith' rather than keeping some 'off the table' to ensure that your preferred solution looks good (2019: 66; 90–1). In that context, new issues arise, such as the need to be beware that new ideas are not backed by evidence of success, or 'best practice' ideas that have been applied only at a smaller scale or in a very different jurisdiction (2019: 70).

Use Political Goals and Value Judgements to Compare Alternatives

The evaluation of each potential solution is necessarily normative. It requires value judgements to decide which solution will produce the 'best' outcome, so recognise the political nature of policy evaluation based on your measures to determine success (see also Compton and 't Hart 2019; McConnell 2010; Ostrom 2011). Typical measures relate to many quite-vague values to which analysts need to attach greater meaning, including: efficiency, equity and fairness, the trade-off between individual freedom and collective action, the extent to which a policy process involves citizens in deliberation, and the impact on a policymaker's popularity (Bardach 2012). Therefore, one pragmatic solution is to focus on the outcomes that key actors care about, such as value for money (Bardach 2012). If so, establish if your solutions will meet an agreed threshold of effectiveness in terms of spending, or present many scenarios based on changing your assumptions underpinning each prediction (Bardach 2012).

'Prescription' methods help provide a consistent way to compare each potential solution, in terms of its feasibility and predicted outcome, combined with normative assessment (Dunn 2017: 55; 190–2; 220–42). Some aspects of assessment are, at first, technical. For example, 'comprehensiveness' describes how many people, and how much of their behaviour, you can influence while minimising the 'burden' on people, businesses, or government (Meltzer and Schwartz 2019: 113–4), while 'mutual exclusiveness' regards the extent to which different objectives do the same thing (2019: 114). However, evaluation is primarily about the choice between normative criteria such as:

1. *Effectiveness.* The size of a policy's intended impact on the problem (2019: 117). Or, the impact of an institution on social and economic life, such as a level of political stability (Mintrom 2012: 49).
2. *Equity (fairness).* The impact in terms of 'vertical equity' (e.g. the better off should pay more), 'horizontal equity' (e.g. you should not pay more if unmarried), fair process, fair outcomes, and 'intergenerational' equity (e.g. don't impose higher costs on future populations) (2019: 118–19).
3. *Feasibility (administrative, technical).* The likelihood of this policy being adopted and implemented well (2019: 119–21).
4. *Cost (or financial feasibility).* Who would bear the cost, and their willingness and ability to pay (2019: 122).
5. *Efficiency.* To maximise the benefit while minimising costs (2019: 122–3). Governments can promote 'efficient' policies by (a) producing the largest number of winners and (b) compensating losers (Mintrom 2012: 51–2). Or, define efficiency in relation to (a) the number of outputs per input and/or (b) a measurable or predictable gain in outcomes, such as 'quality-adjusted life years' in a population (Weimer and Vining 2017: 25–6).
6. *Sustainability.* Such as when governments prioritise environmental sustainability to mitigate climate change (Mintrom 2012: 52–7).
7. The protection of human rights and 'human flourishing' (Mintrom 2012: 52–7).

For Weimer and Vining (2017: 25–6), we should treat values as self-evident goals. They exist alongside the 'instrumental goals'—such as 'sustainable public finance or political feasibility'—necessary to generate support for policy solutions. Further, effective analysis requires us to reduce the cognitive load of policymakers when comparing each option's benefits in relation to different criteria. So, explain potential solutions in sufficient detail to predict the costs and benefits of each 'alternative' (including current policy), and compare specific and well-worked alternatives, such as from 'academic policy researchers' or 'advocacy organisations'.

When explaining objectives and criteria, 'label' your criteria in relation to your policy objectives (e.g. to 'maximise debt reduction') rather than using generic terms (Meltzer and Schwartz 2019: 123–7). Produce a table—with alternatives in rows and criteria in columns—to compare each option, and quantify your policies' likely outcomes, such as in relation to numbers of people affected and levels of income transfer, or a percentage drop in the size of the problem. Consider making a preliminary recommendation to inform an iterative process, drawing feedback from clients and stakeholder groups (2019: 212).

Some Values and Methods Seem to Dominate Policy Analysis

Efficiency and effectiveness tend to be prioritised values, and analyses of each include:

1. *Cost-benefit analysis* (CBA) to (a) identify the most efficient outcomes by (b) translating all of the predicted impacts of an alternative into a single unit of analysis (such as a dollar amount), on the assumption (c) that we can produce winners from policy *and* compensate losers (often known as the Kaldor-Hicks compensation criterion) (Weimer and Vining 2017: 352–5, 398–434).
   - CBA is a dominant but problematic economics method based on the idea that one metric—such as a $ value—can be used to predict and compare outcomes (2017: 209–17).
   - The principle of CBA may be intuitive, and it can help to identify (a) the financial and opportunity cost of your plans (what would you achieve if you spent the money elsewhere?), compared to (b) the positive impact of your funded policy (Meltzer and Schwartz 2019: 141–55).
   - However, a thorough CBA process is resource-intensive, vulnerable to bias and error, and no substitute for choice. It requires you to make a collection of assumptions about human behaviour and likely costs and benefits, decide whose costs and benefits should count, turn all costs and benefits into a single measure, and imagine how to maximise winners and compensate losers (2019: 155–8)
2. *Cost-effectiveness analysis* (CEA). One alternative is CEA, which quantifies costs and relates them to outputs (e.g. number of people affected, and how) without trying to translate them into a single measure of benefit (2019: 181–3; Dunn 2017: 217–9)

3. *Public agency strategic analysis* (PASA) to identify ways in which public organisations can change to provide more benefits with the same resources (Weimer and Vining 2017: 435–50; see O'Flynn 2007 on benefits such as 'public value').

These measures can be combined with other thought processes, such as with reference to 'moral imperatives', a 'precautionary approach', and ethical questions on power/powerlessness (Meltzer and Schwartz 2019: 183–4). Mintrom (2012: 21) emphasises 'prior knowledge and experience' and 'synthesising' work by others alongside techniques such as cost-benefit analyses. Further, while such methods help us combine information and values to compare choices, note the inescapable role of power to decide whose values and which outcomes, affecting whom, matter (Dunn 2017: 204). Policy benefits some social groups more than others.

Be Efficient and Pragmatic When Gathering Evidence

Dunn (2017: 4) describes policy analysis as pragmatic and eclectic. It involves synthesising usable and policy-relevant knowledge (see Lindblom and Cohen 1979) and combining it with experience and 'practical wisdom', to help solve problems with analysis that people can trust. This exercise is 'descriptive', to define problems, and 'normative', to decide how the world should be and how solutions get us there.

Weimer and Vining (2017) suggest that, *ideally*, you would have the time and resources to (a) produce new research and/or (b) 'conduct a meta-analysis' of relevant evaluations to (c) provide 'confident assessments of impacts' and 'engage in highly touted evidence-based policy making'. However, 'short deadlines' and limited access to 'directly relevant data' prompt you to patch together existing research that does not answer your question directly (2017: 327–39; 409–11). Consequently, 'your predictions of the impacts of a unique policy alternative must necessarily be guided by logic and theory, rather than systematic empirical evidence' (2017: 27) and 'we must balance sometimes inconsistent evidence to reach conclusions about appropriate assertions' (2017: 328). This pragmatism extends to identifying the potential to adopt and tailor generic policy instruments (2017: 205–58), 'borrowing' proposals or models from credible sources, and 'tinkering' (using only the relevant elements of a proposal) to make sure they are relevant to your problem (2017: 26–7; 359).

In other words, gather relevant data efficiently, to reflect resource constraints such as time pressures, and think about which data are essential and when you can substitute estimation for research (Bardach 2012). Meltzer and Schwartz (2019: 231–2) describe policy analysis as applied research, drawing on many sources of evidence, quickly, with limited time, access to scientific research, or funding to conduct a lot of new research (2019: 231–2). However, they seem more ambitious than Bardach (and perhaps the others), since analysis requires careful analysis of a wide range of policy-relevant documents (including the 'grey' literature often produced by governments, NGOs, and think tanks—Davidson 2017) and available datasets, perhaps combined with expert interviews, focus groups, site visits, or an online survey (2019: 232–64).

Communicate Clearly and Concisely

Bardach (2012) suggests that communicating with a client requires coherence, clarity, brevity, and minimal jargon. So, identify your target audience and tailor your case, and weigh up the benefits of oral versus written presentation. Quantify and visualise your predictions if possible. Ask yourself if this is such a good solution, why hasn't it been done already (2012)? This emphasis on clarity and brevity is a feature of each text (Mintrom 2012: 82–6, and Weimer and Vining 2017: 23; 370–4).

For Dunn (2017: 19–21; 348–54; 392) 'policy argumentation' and the 'communication of policy-relevant knowledge' are central to policymaking. He identifies seven elements of a 'policy argument' (2017: 19–21; 348–54), including (a) the claim itself, such as a *description* (size, cause) or *evaluation* (importance, urgency) of a problem, and *prescription* of a solution, (b) what supports the claim (including reasoning, knowledge, authority), and (c) what could undermine it. Then, the key stages of communication (2017: 392–7; 405; 432) include:

1. 'Analysis', focusing on the 'technical quality' of the information, and whether it meets client expectations, challenges the 'status quo', and suggests that something can be done.
2. 'Documentation', focusing on synthesising information from many sources, organising it into a coherent argument, translating from jargon or a technical language, simplifying, summarising, and producing user-friendly visuals.
3. 'Utilisation', by making sure that (a) communications are tailored to the audience (its size, existing knowledge of policy and methods, attitude to analysts, and openness to challenge) and (b) the process is 'interactive' to help analysts and their audiences learn from each other.

A 'General Method of Communicating in a Policy Process'

Smith (2015) goes further to note that, in government, policy analysts often write (1) *on behalf of* policymakers, projecting a specific viewpoint, and (2) *for* policymakers, requiring them to (a) work remarkably quickly to (b) produce concise reports to (c) reflect the need to process information efficiently. Actors outside government are less constrained by (1), but still need to write in a similar way. Their audience makes quick judgements on presentations: the source of information, its relevance, and if they should read it fully. Smith's (2015) 'General Method of Communicating in a Policy Process' identifies the questions to ask yourself when communicating policy analysis, summarised as follows.

Step 1: Prepare

- To what policy do I refer?
- Which audiences are relevant?
- What is the political context and the major sites of agreement/disagreement?
- How do I frame the problem, and which stories are relevant to my audience?

Step 2: Plan

- What is this communication's purpose?
- What is my story and message?
- What is my role and interest?
- 'For whom does this communication speak?'
- Who is my audience?
- What will they learn?
- What is the context and timeframe?
- What should be the form, content, and tone of the communication?

Step 3. Produce

- Make a full draft, seek comments during a review, then revise.

Smith (2015) provides two 'checklists' to assess such communications:

1. *Effectiveness.* Speak with an audience in mind, highlight a well-defined problem and purpose, project authority, and use the right form of communication.
2. *Excellence.* Focus on clarity, precision, conciseness, and credibility.

Smith (2015) then focuses on specific aspects of this general method, including:

- *Framing* involves describing the nature of the problem—its scope, and who is affected—and connecting this definition to current or new solutions.
- *Evaluation* requires critical skills to question 'conventional wisdom' and assess the selective use of information by others. Use the 'general method' to ask how others frame problems and solutions, then provide a fresh perspective.
- *Know the Record* involves researching previous solutions. This process reflects the importance of 'precedent': telling a story of previous attempts to solve the problem helps provide context for new debates (and project your knowledgeability).

- *Know the Arguments* involves engaging with the ideas of your allies and competitors. Understand your own position, make a reasoned argument in relation to others, present a position paper, establish its scope (the big picture or specific issue), and think strategically (and ethically) about how to maximise its impact in current debates.
- *Inform Policymakers* suggests maximising policymaker interest by keeping communication concise, polite, and tailored to a policymaker's values and interests.
- *Public Comment* focuses on the importance of working with administrative officials even after legislation is passed (especially if 'street-level bureaucrats' make policy as they deliver—Lipsky 1980; Tummers et al. 2015).

Communicate Risk and Uncertainty in a Responsible and Ethical Way

It is difficult to monitor policy outcomes, far less predict them. Even the most effective methods to extrapolate from the past are flawed, and it is important to communicate levels of uncertainty (Dunn 2017: 118–23).

'Monitoring' methods help identify levels of compliance with regulations if resources and services reach 'target groups', if money is spent correctly (such as on clearly defined 'inputs' such as public sector wages), and if we can make a causal link between the policy inputs/activities/outputs and outcomes (2017: 56; 251–5). Monitoring is crucial because it is so difficult to predict policy success, and unintended consequences are almost inevitable (2017: 250). However, the data gathered are usually no more than proxy indicators of outcomes. Further, the choice of indicators reflect what is *available* rather than necessarily valuable (note the tale of the 'drunkard's search' in Hogwood 1992), 'particular social values', and 'the political biases of analysts' (Dunn 2017: 262)

These problems of monitoring solutions pale into significance with problems of predicting them. As Spiegelhalter (2018) describes, there is continuous scientific uncertainty about the ability of our data to give us accurate knowledge of the world, such as when:

1. We use a survey of a sample population, in the hope that (a) respondents provide accurate answers, and (b) their responses provide a representative picture of the population we seek to understand. In such cases, professional standards and practices exist to *minimise, but not remove* biases associated with questions and sampling (Spiegelhalter 2018: 74).
2. Some people ignore (and other people underestimate) the 'margin of error' in surveys, even though they could be larger than the reported change in data (2018: 189–92; 247).
3. Alternatives to surveys have major unintended consequences, such as when government statistics are collected unsystematically or otherwise misrepresent outcomes (2018: 84–5).
4. 'Correlation does not equal causation' (see also Pearl and Mackenzie 2019).
   - The cause of an association between two things could be either of those things, or another thing (Spiegelhalter 2018: 95–9; 110–15).
   - It is usually prohibitively expensive to conduct and analyse research to minimise doubt, such as by using multiple 'randomised control trials' to establish cause and effect in the same ways as medicines trials (2018: 104).
   - Further, our complex and uncontrolled world is not as conducive to the experimental trials of social and economic policies.
5. The misleading *appearance* of a short-term trend often relates to 'chance variation' rather than a long-term trend (e.g. in PISA education tables or crime rates—2018: 131; 249).
6. The algorithms used to process huge amounts of data may contain unhelpful rules and misplaced assumptions that bias the results, and this problem is worse if the rules are kept secret (2018: 178–87).
7. Calculating the probability of events is difficult to *do*, agree *how to do*, and *to understand* (2018: 216–20; 226; 239; 304–7).
8. The likelihood of identifying 'false positive' results in research is high (2018: 278–80). Note the comparison to finding someone guilty when innocent, or innocent when guilty (2018: 284 and compare with Gigerenzer 2015: 33–7; 161–8). However, the professional incentive to minimise these outcomes or admit the research's limitations is low (2018: 278; 287; 294–302).

How to Communicate Evidence Responsibly

Further, it has become common to use the phrase 'lies, damned lies, and statistics' to suggest that people can manipulate the presentation of information to reinforce whatever case they want to make. Common examples include the highly selective sharing of data, and the use of misleading images to distort the size of an effect or strength of a relationship between 'variables' (when we try to find out if a change in one thing causes a change in another). Spiegelhalter highlights the great potential to mislead, via:

1. deliberate manipulation,
2. a poor grasp of statistics, *and/or*
3. insufficient appreciation of (a) your non-specialist audience's potential reaction to (b) different ways to frame the same information (2018: 354–62), *perhaps based on*
4. the unscientific belief that scientists are objective and can communicate the truth in a neutral way, rather than storytellers with imperfect data (2018: 68–9; 307; 338; 342–53).

Potentially influential communications include (2018: 19–38):

1. The choice of image, with bar or line-based charts often more useful than pie charts (and dynamic often better than static—2018: 71)
2. The point at which you cut off the chart's axis to downplay or accentuate the difference between results
3. Framing the results positively (e.g. survival rate) versus negatively (e.g. death rate)
4. Describing a higher *relative risk* (e.g. 18%) or *absolute risk* (e.g. from 6 in 100 to 7 in 100 cases)
5. Describing risk in relation to decimal places, percentages, or numbers out of 100
6. Using the wrong way to describe an average (mode, median, or mean—2018: 46)
7. Using a language familiar to specialists but confusing to—and subject to misinterpretation by—non-specialists (e.g. odds ratios)
8. Translating numbers into words (e.g. what does 'very likely' mean?) to describe probability (2018: 320).

These problems with the *supply* of information combine with the ways that citizens and policymakers *consume* it. People use cognitive shortcuts, such as emotions and heuristics, to process information. It can make them vulnerable to manipulation, and prompt them to change their behaviour after misinterpreting evidence in relation to risk (2018: 33; Gigerenzer 2015: 2–13; Kahneman 2012).

In that context, your first aim as a policy analyst is to become a skilled consumer of information. Then, you may be asked to gather and present data as part of your policy analysis, and to not mislead people. Therefore, your second aim is to become an ethical and skilled communicator of information. In each case, a good simple rule is to assume that the analysts who help policymakers learn how to consume and interpret evidence are more influential than the researchers who produce it. The technical skill to gather and analyse information is necessary for research, while the skill to communicate findings is necessary to avoid misleading your audience.

Therefore, responsible analysts communicate the degree of uncertainty related to any estimate (Meltzer and Schwartz 2019: 128–32), predict the most likely outcomes of each alternative, while recognising high uncertainty (2019: 189–92). If possible, draw on existing, comparable, programmes to predict the effectiveness of yours (2019: 192–4), combine such analysis with relevant theories to predict human behaviour (e.g. consider price 'elasticity' if you seek to raise the price of a good to discourage its use) (2019: 193–4), apply statistical methods to calculate the probability of each outcome (2019: 195–6), and modify your assumptions to produce a range of possibilities.

What Is Missing from These Policy Analysis 'How to' Guides?

The next three chapters highlight what is missing from such classic analyses, with the first point magnifying the importance of the other two. First, new studies of policy analysis highlight a clear sense of change in the role of policy analysts. The old story of a small group of technocratic analysts, using scientific methods to inform one government directly, has given way to a new story of highly competitive and political analysis across many levels and types of government. Second, this shift in story prompts us to seek a much more comprehensive sense of the wider policymaking context in which analysts operate. Policy analysis texts give us a taste of the policy process, but only specialist research can give us the full meal. Third, these texts also *introduce* the idea that the production and use of policy-relevant knowledge is itself a political act. However, they only scratch the surface of the ways in which we can understand the politics of knowledge and evidence.

REFERENCES

Bardach, E. (2012). *A Practical Guide for Policy Analysis* (4th ed.). CQ Press.
Bardach, E., & Patashnik, E. (2020). *A Practical Guide for Policy Analysis* (6th ed.). (International Student ed.). London: Sage.
Cairney, P., & Kwiatkowski, R. (2017). How to Communicate Effectively with Policymakers: Combine Insights from Psychology and Policy Studies. *Palgrave Communications, 3*, 37. Retrieved from https://www.nature.com/articles/s41599-017-0046-8.
Compton, M., & 't Hart, P. (2019). *Great Policy Successes*. Oxford: Oxford University Press.
Davidson, B. (2017). Storytelling and Evidence-based Policy: Lessons from the Grey Literature. *Palgrave Communications, 3*, 17093. https://doi.org/10.1057/palcomms.2017.93.
Dunn, W. (2017). *Public Policy Analysis* (6th ed.). Routledge.
Gigerenzer, G. (2015). *Risk Savvy*. London: Penguin.
Hogwood, B. (1992). *Trends in British Public Policy*. Buckingham: Open University Press.
John, P. (2018). *How Far to Nudge? Assessing Behavioural Public Policy*. Cheltenham: Edward Elgar.
Kahneman, D. (2012). *Thinking Fast and Slow*. London: Penguin.
Lindblom, C., & Cohen, D. (1979). *Usable Knowledge: Social Science and Social Problem Solving*. New Haven: Yale University Press.
Lipsky, M. (1980). *Street-Level Bureaucracy*. New York: Russell Sage Foundation.
McConnell, A. (2010). *Understanding Policy Success: Rethinking Public Policy*. London: Red Globe Press.
Meltzer, R., & Schwartz, A. (2019). *Policy Analysis as Problem Solving*. London: Routledge.
Mintrom, M. (2012). *Contemporary Policy Analysis*. Oxford: Oxford University Press.

O'Flynn, J. (2007). From New Public Management to Public Value: Paradigmatic Change and Managerial Implications. *Australian Journal of Public Administration, 66*(3), 353–366.

Ostrom, E. (2011). Background on the Institutional Analysis and Development Framework. *Policy Studies Journal, 39*(1), 7–27.

Pearl, J., & Mackenzie, D. (2019). *The Book of Why*. London: Penguin.

Smith, C. (2015). *Writing Public Policy*. Oxford University Press.

Spiegelhalter, D. (2018). *The Art of Statistics: Learning from Data*. London: Pelican.

Tummers, L. L., Bekkers, V., Vink, E., & Musheno, M. (2015). Coping During Public Service Delivery: A Conceptualization and Systematic Review of the Literature. *Journal of Public Administration Research and Theory, 25*(4), 1099–1126.

Weimer, D., & Vining, A. (2017). *Policy Analysis: Concepts and Practice* (6th ed.). London: Routledge.

CHAPTER 3

What Has Changed, and Why Do We Need New Policy Analysis?

Abstract This chapter explains old and new stories of policy analysis. Classic policy analysis texts highlight the client-oriented nature of policy analysis, but within a changing policy process that has altered the nature of that relationship profoundly. A new policymaking environment requires new policy analysis styles, skills, and training.

Keywords Policy analysis • Policy analysts • Rational policymaking • Comparative policy analysis • Policy analysis styles • Policymaking complexity

INTRODUCTION

Classic texts highlight the client-oriented nature of policy analysis, but within a changing policy process that has altered the nature of that relationship profoundly. This new policymaking environment requires new policy analysis skills and training (Mintrom 2012) and limits the applicability of classic five-step policy analysis techniques. As Radin (2019: 2) describes, 'The basic relationship between a decision-maker (the client) and an analyst has moved from a two-person encounter to an extremely complex and diverse set of interactions'.

To demonstrate, we can use Radin's work on the history of US policy analysis to produce simple stories about old and new policy analysis.

© The Author(s), under exclusive license to Springer Nature
Switzerland AG 2021
P. Cairney, *The Politics of Policy Analysis*,
https://doi.org/10.1007/978-3-030-66122-9_3

Although Radin is describing one political system, these stories are supported by comparative studies of policy analysis (Brans et al. 2017) and policy research (see Chap. 4).

Story 1: The Old Ways of Making Policy Were Centralised, Exclusive, and Focused on Problem-Solving

Policy analysis took place in an environment that resembled a club (Heclo 1978: 94), in which there was a powerful centre or clear sense of a federal government hierarchy. As such, there was a small number of analysts, generally inside government (such as senior bureaucrats, economists, or scientific experts), giving technical or factual advice, about policy formulation, to policymakers at the heart of government, on the assumption that policy problems would be solved via analysis and action.

Story 2: Modern Policy Analysis Is More Open and Politicised, and the Focus Is Less Certain

Now, there are many analysts, inside and outside government. They compete with other actors to interpret facts, find an audience, and give advice. Advice can be about setting the agenda, making, delivering, and evaluating policy. It extends across many policymaking venues. Further, governments have a limited ability to understand and solve the complex policy problems described in policy analyses. As Enserink et al. (2013: 13–6) describe, historic attempts to seek 'rational' policy analysis enjoy limited success because policymaking complexity is 'more in line with political reality'. Table 3.1 summarises this shift in focus.

Radin describes an increasingly fluid client-analyst relationship. In previous eras, the analyst's client was a senior policymaker, the main focus was on the analyst-client relationship, and 'both analysts and clients did not spend much time or energy thinking about the dimensions of the policy environment in which they worked' (2019: 59). Now, in a multi-centric policymaking environment, three main problems arise.

First, it is relatively difficult to identify the client. We could imagine the client to be someone paying for the analysis, someone affected by its recommendations, or all policy actors with the ability to act on the advice (2019: 10). If there is 'shared authority' for policymaking within one

Table 3.1 Policy analysis in the 'rational' and real world

	'Rational' policy analysis	*Analysis in the real world*
Number of actors	Centralised process with few actors inside government	Messy process, with many policymakers and influencers, inside and outside government
Role of knowledge	Translating science into policy	A competition to frame issues and assess policy-relevant knowledge
Finding solutions	An 'optimal' solution from one perspective	A negotiated solution based on many perspectives (in which optimality is contested)
Relevant skills	Analysing a policy problem and solution with one metric (e.g. cost-benefit analysis)	Developing new skills including stakeholder analysis, network management, collaboration, mediation, or conflict resolution

Source: Author's own, adapted from text in Enserink et al. (2013: 17–34)

political system, a 'client' (or *audience*) may be a collection of policymakers and influencers spread across a network containing multiple types of government, non-governmental actors, and actors responsible for policy delivery (2019: 33). The growth in international cooperation also complicates the idea of a single client for policy advice (2019: 33–4). This shift may limit the 'face-to-face encounters' that would otherwise provide information for—and perhaps trust in—the analyst (2019: 2–3).

Second, it is relatively difficult to identify the analyst. Radin (2019: 9–25) traces a major expansion of policy analysts, from the notional centre of policymaking in federal government towards analysts spread across many venues, inside government (across multiple levels, 'policy units', and government agencies), in congressional committees, and outside government (such as in influential think tanks). Policy analysts can also be specialist external companies contracted by organisations to provide advice (2019: 37–8).

This expansion shifted the image of analysts, from a small number of trusted insiders towards many being treated as akin to interest groups selling their pet policies (2019: 25–6). The nature of policy analysis has always been a bit vague, but now it seems more common to suggest that 'policy analysts' may really be 'policy advocates' (2019: 44–6). As such, they may have to work harder to demonstrate their usefulness (2019: 80–1) and accept that their analysis will have a limited direct impact (2019: 82).

Third, consequently, the required skills of policy analysis—and the image of analysts—have changed. Although many people value systematic policy analysis, an effective analyst does not simply apply economic or scientific techniques to analyse a problem or solution, or rely on one source of expertise or method, as if it were possible to provide 'neutral information' (2019: 26).

Radin (2019: 31; 48) compares the old 'acceptance that analysts would be governed by the norms of neutrality and objectivity' with increasing calls to acknowledge that policy analysis is part of a political project to foster some notion of public good or 'public interest'. The *projection* of reason and neutrality is a political strategy, but it relies on fictional divide between political policymakers and neutral analysts that is difficult to maintain.

Rather, think of analysts as developing wider skills to operate in a highly political environment in which the nature of the policy issue is contested, responsibility for a policy problem is unclear, and it is not clear how to resolve major debates on values and priorities. Some analysts will be expected to see the problem from the perspective of a specific client with a particular agenda. Other analysts may be valued for their flexibility and pragmatism, such as when they acknowledge the role of their own values, maintain or operate within networks, communicate by many means, and supplement 'quantitative data' with 'hunches' when required (2019: 2–3; 28–9).

COMPARATIVE STUDIES OF POLICY ANALYSIS TELL THE SAME STORY

While Radin describes these dynamics in the US, wider comparative studies confirm and magnify a need to identify, 'the science, art and craft of policy analysis in different countries, at different levels of government and by all relevant actors in and outside government who contribute to the analysis of problems and the search for policy solutions' (Brans et al. 2017: 1). Indeed, Brans et al.'s (2017: 1–6) opening discussion suggests that the task of policy analysis is generally unclear. They highlight the following issues:

1. *The scope of policy analysis is wide, and its meaning unclear.* Analysts can be found in many levels and types of government, in bodies

holding governments to account, and organisations outside of government, including interest groups, think tanks, and specialist firms such as global accountancy or management consultancy firms (Saint-Martin 2017). Further, 'what counts' as policy analysis can relate to the people that do it, the rules they follow, the processes in which they engage, the form of outputs, and the expectations of clients (Veselý 2017: 103; Vining and Boardman 2017: 264).

2. *The role of a policy analyst varies remarkably in relation to context.* It varies over time, policy area, type of government (such as central, subnational, local), country, type of political system (such as majoritarian or consensus democracies), and 'policy style' (Howlett and Tosun 2019).

3. *Analysis involves 'science, art, and craft'* and *the rules are written and unwritten.* The processes of policy analysis—such as to gather and analyse information, define problems, design and compare solutions, and give policy advice—include 'applied social and scientific research as well as more implicit forms of practical knowledge', and 'both formal and informal professional practices'.

4. *The policy process is complex.* It is difficult to identify a straightforward process in which analysts are clearly engaged in multiple, well-defined, 'stages' of policymaking.

5. *Key principles and practices can be institutionalised, contested, or non-existent.* The idea of policy analysis principles—'of transparency, effectiveness, efficiency and accountability through systematic and evidence-based analysis'—may be entrenched in places like the US but not globally. The existence of major variations across political systems warns us against a tendency to equate US (or West European) analysis as universal.

In *some* political systems (particularly in the 'Anglo-Saxon family of nations') the following forms of policy analysis are taken for granted: scholars encourage or criticise five-step policy analysis techniques; methods such as cost-benefit analysis are institutionalised and difficult to replace or supplement with other techniques; and, there is high rhetorical commitment to the idea of 'evidence-based policymaking' (Brans et al. 2017: 4–5; Cairney 2016). Even so, the status of science and expertise is often contested, particularly in relation to salient and polarised issues, or more generally:

- During 'attempts by elected politicians to restore the primacy of political judgement in the policymaking process, at the expense of technical or scientific evidence' (Brans et al. 2017: 5).
- When the 'blending of expert policy analysis with public consultation and participation' makes 'advice more competitive and contested' (2017: 5).
- When evidence-based really means evidence-informed, given that there are many legitimate claims to knowledge, and evidence forms one part of a larger process of policy design (van Nispen and de Jong 2017: 153; Boaz et al. 2019).

In *many* political systems, there may be less criticism of the idea of 'systematic and evidence-based analysis' because there is less capacity to process information. It is difficult to worry about excessively technocratic approaches if they do not exist.

Policy Analysis as a Collection of Styles, Not One Analytical Approach

Under these circumstances, it is difficult to think of policy analysis as a profession with a clearly defined role and common reference point. Rather, it seems increasingly to be a loosely defined collection of practices that vary according to context. As such, we can consider policy analysis to be a collection of 'styles' that can be described empirically or prescribed for practice.

First, Brans et al.'s (2017) edited volume contains a rich empirical account, in which Hassenteufel and Zittoun (2017) identify a collection of 'styles' influenced by many factors. Sources of variation include: competing analytical approaches in different political systems (2017: 65); levels of bureaucratic capacity for analysis (Mendez and Dussauge-Laguna 2017: 82); the extent to which policymakers contract out analysis (Veselý 2017: 113); the types and remits of advisory bodies (e.g. do they simply offer advice, or also foster wider participation to generate knowledge? Crowley and Head 2017); the level of government in which analysts work, such as 'subnational' (Newman 2017) or 'local' (Lundin and Öberg 2017); and the type of activity, such as when economic methods and 'new public management' reforms influence 'performance budgeting analysis' (van Nispen and de Jong 2017: 143–52).

Policy analysis can also describe a remarkably wide range of activity, including: public inquiries (Marier 2017); advice to MPs, parliaments, and their committees (Wolfs and De Winter 2017); the strategic analysis of public opinion or social media data (Rothmayr Allison 2017; Kuo and Cheng 2017); a diverse set of activities associated with 'think tanks' (Stone and Ladi 2017) and 'political party think tanks' (Pattyn et al. 2017); analysis for and by 'business associations' (Vining and Boardman 2017), unions (Schulze and Schroeder 2017), and voluntary/non-profit organisations (Evans et al. 2017), all of whom juggle policy advice to government with keeping members on board; and the more-or-less policy-relevant work of academic researchers (Blum and Brans 2017; see also Cairney and Oliver 2018; Oliver and Cairney 2019).

Second, Thissen and Walker's (2013) edited volume adds a prescriptive element to their studies, in which: 'Our premise is that there is no single, let alone "one best", way of conducting policy analyses' (Thissen and Walker 2013: 2). They begin by identifying the proliferation of policy analysts inside and outside government, the many approaches and methods that could count as policy analysis, and therefore a proliferation of concepts to describe it. Further, they show that policy process research informs our understanding of policy analysis, since it is difficult to know what analysts and their clients *should* do unless we know what they *can* do.

As Enserink et al. (2013: 12–3) describe, policy analysis will change profoundly if the policy process is 'chaotic and messy' rather than 'neat and rational' (see Table 3.1). Or, the role of a policy analyst will change according to the type of political exchange they address. While 'rational' analysis involves answering a question for a client, other roles include providing persuasive narratives to help build alliances, or analysing institutional and policy processes to identify likely obstacles to policy change (2013: 35).

In that context, rather than identify a five-step plan for policy analysis, Mayer et al. (2013: 43–50) suggest that policy analysts could combine one or more of six activities:

1. 'Research and analyse', to collect information relevant to policy problems.
2. 'Design and recommend', to produce a range of potential solutions.
3. 'Clarify values and arguments', to identify potential conflicts and facilitate high-quality debate.

4. 'Advise strategically', to help a policymaker choose an effective solution within their political context.
5. 'Democratise', to pursue a 'normative and ethical objective: it should further equal access to, and influence on, the policy process for all stakeholders' (2013: 47).
6. 'Mediate', to foster many forms of cooperation between governments, stakeholders (including business), researchers, and/or citizens.

Policy analysts would not perform these functions sequentially or with equal weight. Rather, Mayer et al. (2013: 50–5) describe 'six styles of policy analysis' that will vary according to the analyst's 'assumptions about science (epistemology), democracy, learning, and change':

1. *Rational*, based on the idea that we can conduct research in a straightforward way within a well-ordered policy process (or modify the analysis to reflect limits to research).
2. *Argumentative*, based on a competition to define policy problems and solutions.
3. *Client advice*, based on the assumption that analysis is part of a 'political game', and analysts bring knowledge of political strategy and policymaking complexity.
4. *Participatory*, to facilitate more equal access to information and debate among citizens.
5. *Process*, based on the idea that the faithful adherence to good procedures aids high-quality analysis (and perhaps mitigates an 'erratic and volatile' policy process).
6. *Interactive*, based on the idea that the rehearsal of many competing perspectives is useful to policymaker deliberations (compare with Dunlop and Radaelli 2013 on reflexive learning).

In turn, these styles prompt different questions to evaluate the activities associated with analysis (2013: 56). The criteria for 'good' policy analysis include the quality of knowledge, usefulness of advice to clients and stakeholders, quality of argumentation, pragmatism of advice, transparency of processes, and ability to secure a mediated settlement (2013: 58). The positive role for analysts includes 'independent scientist' or expert, 'ethicist', 'narrator', 'counsellor', 'entrepreneur',' democratic advocate', or 'facilitator' (2013: 59). Or, different styles—appealing to scientific evidence or argumentation—inform policy design processes, designed to change people's minds during repeated interactions between analysts and clients (Bots 2013: 114).

This discussion of styles informs problem definition within complex policymaking systems. For example, compare (a) a 'rational' approach relying on research knowledge to diagnose problems, with (b) a 'political game model' emphasising key actors and their perspectives, value conflicts, trust, interdependence, and the varying potential to make deals (Thissen 2013: 66–9). These different starting points influence the ways in which analysts might take steps to identify: how people perceive policy problems, if other definitions are more useful; how to identify a problem's cause and effect, and the likely effect of a proposed solution; how to communicate uncertainty; and how to relate the results to a 'policy arena' with its own rules on resolving conflict and producing policy instruments (2013: 70–84; 93–4).

They also intersect with categories of policy problems, including 'tamed' (high knowledge/technically solvable, with no political conflict); 'untamed ethical/political' (technically solvable, with high moral and political conflict); 'untamed scientific' (high consensus but low scientific knowledge); and 'untamed' problems (low consensus, low knowledge) (Bruijn et al. 2013: 134–5). Put simply, 'rational' approaches may help address tamed issues, while other skills are required to manage processes—such as conflict resolution and stakeholder engagement—associated with untamed issues (2013: 136–40). In complex systems, analysts focus less on 'unilateral decisions using command and control' and more on 'consultation and negotiation among stakeholders' in networks. The latter are necessary because there will always be contestation about what the available information tells us about the problem, often without a simple way to agree choices on solutions.

Therefore, although there exist some useful five-step guides for budding analysts, analysts also need to find ways to understand and engage with a complex policymaking system containing a huge number of analysts, policymakers, and influencers. Mayer et al.'s (2013: 60) visualisations of these roles project the sense that (a) individuals face a trade-off between roles (even if they seek to combine some) and (b) many people making many trade-offs adds up to a complex picture of activity.

IMPLICATIONS FOR POLICY ANALYSIS AND PROFESSIONAL DEVELOPMENT: RADIN'S SKILLS CHECKLIST

This discussion has major implications for the idea of policy analysis training. When discussing a previous era, Geva-May (2005: 15) describes a profession with its own set of practices and ways of thinking. As with professions like medicine, it would be unwise to practice policy analysis without education and training or otherwise learning the 'craft' shared by a policy analysis community (2005: 16–17). For example, policy analysts can draw on five-step processes to diagnose a policy problem and potential solutions (2005: 18–21). Analysts may also combine these steps with heuristics to determine the technical and political feasibility of their proposals (2005: 22–5), as they address inevitable uncertainty and their own bounded rationality (2005: 26–34). Some aspects of the role—such as research methods and techniques such as cost-benefit analysis—can be taught in graduate programmes, while others may be better suited to on the job learning (2005: 36–40). If so, policy analysis practices reflect different cultures in each political system, but within a profession that guides the development of core skills and assumptions.

However, if it is difficult to think of policy analysis as a profession, we may wonder if policy analysis can ever be based on common skills and methods (such as described by Scott 2017), connected to 'formal education and training', 'a code of professional conduct', and the ability of organisations to control membership (Adachi 2017: 28). Put simply, we should not assume that graduates in policy analysis will enter a central government with high capacity, coherent expectations, and a clear demand for their skills. Yet, Fukuyama (2018) argues that US university programmes largely teach students:

> a battery of quantitative methods ... applied econometrics, cost-benefit analysis, decision analysis, and, most recently, use of randomized experiments for program evaluation ... [that] will tell you what the optimal policy should be ... [but not] how to achieve that outcome. The world is littered with optimal policies that don't have a snowball's chance in hell of being adopted.

Fukuyama (2018) argues for the value of other key skills. They include stakeholder mapping, to identify who is crucial to policy success, defining policy problems in a way that stakeholders and policymakers can support, and including those actors continuously during a process of policy design and delivery. Compare with Botha et al. (2017), who suggest that the policy analysis programmes across North American and European universities offer a more diverse range of skills, and support for experiential learning, than Fukuyama describes.

Such discussions serve two main functions. First, they contrast with the idea that we can simply break policy analysis into five steps. Second, they describe policy analysis as an almost overwhelming task with no guarantee of policy impact. This cautious, eyes-wide-open, approach may be preferable to the sense that policy analysts can change the world if they just get the evidence and the steps right. Further, a more ambitious hope may be that policy actors focus more on the *process* of policy analysis, such as to widen what we mean by policy-relevant knowledge and focus on long-term collaboration over (rather elusive) short-term impact.

Radin (2019: 21) emphasises this shift in approach as follows. The idea of producing new and relatively abstract ideas, based on high control over available scientific information, at the top of a hierarchical organisation, makes way for a huge list of skills that analysts may find useful in a more complex environment. They include to:

- generate a wide understanding of organisational and policy processes, to reflect the diffusion of power across multiple policy-making venues
- identify a map of stakeholders
- manage networks of policymakers and influencers
- incorporate 'multiple and often conflicting perspectives'
- make and deliver more concrete proposals (2019: 59–74).

Radin's (2019: 48) overall list of relevant skills is huge, including:

Case study methods, Cost-benefit analysis, Ethical analysis, Evaluation, Futures analysis, Historical analysis, Implementation analysis, Interviewing, Legal analysis, Microeconomics, Negotiation, mediation, Operations research, Organizational analysis, Political feasibility analysis, Public speaking, Small-group facilitation, Specific program knowledge, Statistics, Survey research methods, Systems analysis.

They develop alongside analytical *experience* and status, from the early career analyst trying to secure or keep a job, to the experienced operator looking forward to retirement (2019: 54–5). Based on these skills requirements, the contested nature of evidence, and the complexity of the policymaking environment, Radin (2019: 128–31) produces a four-page checklist of 91 questions for policy analysts.

Similarly, Thissen and Walker's (2013) edited volume identifies a wide range of possibilities for policy analysis, including:

1. Walker and van Daalen (2013: 157–84) explore models designed to compare the status quo with a future state, often based on the (shaky) assumption that the world is knowable and we can predict with sufficient accuracy the impact of policy solutions.
2. Hermans and Cunningham (2013: 185–213) describe models to trace agent behaviour in networks and systems, and create multiple possible scenarios, which could help explore the 'implementability' of policies.
3. Walker et al. (2013: 215–61) relate policy analysis styles to how analysts might deal with inevitable uncertainty. Some models serve to reduce 'epistemic' uncertainty associated with insufficient knowledge about the future (perhaps with a focus on methods and statistical analysis). Others focus on resolving ambiguity, in which many actors define problems and feasible solutions in different ways.

The length of these lists, and range of possibilities, reflects the complexity of policy analysis in practice. The nature of information, and the practices used to gather it, is contested (Radin 2019: 89–103). There are major limits to a government's ability to understand and solve the problems described (2019: 95–6). There are inescapable conflicts over trade-offs between solutions achieving different values and goals (2019: 105–8). Policy processes exhibit major variations according to the problem, levels of policymaker attention, and relationships within networks across different policy sectors and notional 'stages' of policymaking (2019: 75–9; 84). Five-step analysis models represent a pragmatic response to such complexity, but also downplay its importance and inflate expectations for impact.

The Inextricable Link Between the Analysis of and for Policy

Under these circumstances, it is difficult to maintain a separation between the analysis *for* policy from the analysis *of* policymaking (described by, e.g. Vining and Weimer 2010; Thissen and Walker 2013: 4). When defining policy analysis largely as a collection of highly variable practices, in complex policymaking systems, we can see the symbiotic relationship between policy analysis and policy research. Studying policy analysis allows us to generate knowledge of policy processes, and policy process research demonstrates that the policymaking context influences how we think about policy analysis. Technical models for policy analysis lack value without clarity about (a) our beliefs regarding the nature of policymaking and (b) the styles of analysis we should use to resolve policy problems, and few of these initial choices can be resolved with reference to scientific analysis or evidence (Thissen and Walker 2013). Therefore, the next chapter examines the insights from policy process research that policy analysts need to know, while chapters in part two compare insights from both approaches (see, e.g. Chap. 7).

References

Adachi, Y. (2017). The Policy Analysis Profession. In M. Brans, I. Geva-May, & M. Howlett (Eds.), *Routledge Handbook of Comparative Policy Analysis* (pp. 27–42). London: Routledge.

Blum, S., & Brans, M. (2017). Academic Policy Analysis and Research Utilization in Policymaking. In M. Brans, I. Geva-May, & M. Howlett (Eds.), *Routledge Handbook of Comparative Policy Analysis* (pp. 341–359). London: Routledge.

Boaz, A., Davies, H., Fraser, A., & Nutley, S. (Eds.). (2019). *What Works Now?* Bristol: Policy Press.

Botha, J., Geva-May, I., & Maslove, A. (2017). Public Policy Studies in North America and Europe. In M. Brans, I. Geva-May, & M. Howlett (Eds.), *Routledge Handbook of Comparative Policy Analysis* (pp. 360–379). London: Routledge.

Bots, P. (2013). Designing the Policy Analysis Process. In W. Thissen & W. Walker (Eds.), *Public Policy Analysis: New Developments* (pp. 103–132). London: Springer.

Brans, M., Geva-May, I., & Howlett, M. (2017). The Policy Analysis Movement: The State of the Art. In M. Brans, I. Geva-May, & M. Howlett (Eds.), *Routledge Handbook of Comparative Policy Analysis*. London: Routledge.

Bruijn, H., ten Heuvlhof, E., & Enserink, B. (2013). Organising the Policy Analysis Process. In W. Thissen & W. Walker (Eds.), *Public Policy Analysis: New Developments* (pp. 133–155). London: Springer.

Cairney, P. (2016). *The Politics of Evidence-based Policymaking*. London: Palgrave Pivot.

Cairney, P., & Oliver, K. (2018). How Should Academics Engage in Policymaking to Achieve Impact? *Political Studies Review*. https://doi.org/10.1177/1478929918807714.

Crowley, K., & Head, B. (2017). Expert Advisory Bodies in The Policy System. In M. Brans, I. Geva-May, & M. Howlett (Eds.), *Routledge Handbook of Comparative Policy Analysis* (pp. 181–198). London: Routledge.

Dunlop, C., & Radaelli, C. (2013). Systematising Policy Learning: From Monolith to Dimensions. *Political Studies Review, 61*(3), 599–619.

Enserink, B., Koppenjan, J., & Mayer, I. (2013). A Policy Sciences View on Policy Analysis. In W. Thissen & W. Walker (Eds.), *Public Policy Analysis: New Developments* (pp. 11–40). London: Springer.

Evans, B., Glass, J., & Wellstead, A. (2017). Policy Analysis and the Voluntary Sector. In M. Brans, I. Geva-May, & M. Howlett (Eds.), *Routledge Handbook of Comparative Policy Analysis* (pp. 291–306). London: Routledge.

Fukuyama, F. (2018). What's Wrong with Public Policy Education. *The American Interest*. Retrieved February 12, 2020, from https://www.the-american-interest.com/2018/08/01/whats-wrong-with-public-policy-education/.

Geva-May, I. (2005). Thinking Like a Policy Analyst. Policy Analysis as a Clinical Profession. In I. Geva-May (Ed.), *Thinking Like a Policy Analyst*. Basingstoke: Palgrave Macmillan.

Hassenteufel, P., & Zittoun, P. (2017). From Policy Analytical Styles to Policymaking Styles. In M. Brans, I. Geva-May, & M. Howlett (Eds.), *Routledge Handbook of Comparative Policy Analysis* (pp. 56–69). London: Routledge.

Heclo, H. (1978). Issue Networks and the Executive Establishment. In A. King (Ed.), *The New American Political System*. Washington, DC: American Enterprise Institute.

Hermans, L., & Cunningham, S. (2013). Actor Models for Policy Analysis. In W. Thissen & W. Walker (Eds.), *Public Policy Analysis: New Developments* (pp. 185–214). London: Springer.

Howlett, M., & Tosun, J. (Eds.). (2019). *Policy Styles and Policy-Making: Exploring the National Dimension*. London: Routledge.

Kuo, Y., & Cheng, M. (2017). Media and Policy Analysis. In M. Brans, I. Geva-May, & M. Howlett (Eds.), *Routledge Handbook of Comparative Policy Analysis* (pp. 309–323). London: Routledge.

Lundin, M., & Öberg, P. (2017). Policy Analysis at the Local Level. In M. Brans, I. Geva-May, & M. Howlett (Eds.), *Routledge Handbook of Comparative Policy Analysis* (pp. 131–142). London: Routledge.

Marier, P. (2017). Public Inquiries. In M. Brans, I. Geva-May, & M. Howlett (Eds.), *Routledge Handbook of Comparative Policy Analysis* (pp. 169–180). London: Routledge.

Mayer, I., van Daalen, C. E., & Bots, P. (2013). Perspectives on Policy Analysis: A Framework for Understanding and Design. In W. Thissen & W. Walker (Eds.), *Public Policy Analysis: New Developments* (pp. 41–64). London: Springer.

Mendez, J., & Dussauge-Laguna, M. (2017). Policy Analysis and Bureaucratic Capacity. In M. Brans, I. Geva-May, & M. Howlett (Eds.), *Routledge Handbook of Comparative Policy Analysis* (pp. 70–84). London: Routledge.

Mintrom, M. (2012). *Contemporary Policy Analysis*. Oxford: Oxford University Press.

Newman, J. (2017). Policy Analysis in Sub-national Governments. In M. Brans, I. Geva-May, & M. Howlett (Eds.), *Routledge Handbook of Comparative Policy Analysis* (pp. 118–130). London: Routledge.

Oliver, K., & Cairney, P. (2019). The Dos and Don'ts of Influencing Policy: A Systematic Review of Advice to Academics. *Palgrave Communications, 5*(21), 1–11.

Pattyn, V., Pittoors, G., & Van Hecke, S. (2017). Who Are the Political Parties' Ideas Factories? On Policy Analysis by Political: Party Think Tanks. In M. Brans, I. Geva-May, & M. Howlett (Eds.), *Routledge Handbook of Comparative Policy Analysis* (pp. 245–260). London: Routledge.

Radin, B. (2019). *Policy Analysis in the Twenty-First Century*. London: Routledge.

Rothmayr Allison, C. (2017). Public Opinion and Policy Analysis. In M. Brans, I. Geva-May, & M. Howlett (Eds.), *Routledge Handbook of Comparative Policy Analysis* (pp. 229–241). London: Routledge.

Saint-Martin, D. (2017). Management Consultancy and the Varieties of Capitalism. In M. Brans, I. Geva-May, & M. Howlett (Eds.), *Routledge Handbook of Comparative Policy Analysis* (pp. 213–228). London: Routledge.

Schulze, M., & Schroeder, W. (2017). Policy Analysis by the Labour Movement: A Comparative Analysis of Labour Market Policy in Germany, Denmark and The United States. In M. Brans, I. Geva-May, & M. Howlett (Eds.), *Routledge Handbook of Comparative Policy Analysis* (pp. 276–290). London: Routledge.

Scott, C. (2017). The Choice of Formal Policy Analysis Method. In M. Brans, I. Geva-May, & M. Howlett (Eds.), *Routledge Handbook of Comparative Policy Analysis* (pp. 43–55). London: Routledge.

Stone, D., & Ladi, S. (2017). Policy Analysis and Think Tanks in Comparative Perspective. In M. Brans, I. Geva-May, & M. Howlett (Eds.), *Routledge Handbook of Comparative Policy Analysis* (pp. 324–340). London: Routledge.

Thissen, W. (2013). Diagnosing Policy Problem Situations. In W. Thissen & W. Walker (Eds.), *Public Policy Analysis: New Developments* (pp. 65–102). London: Springer.

Thissen, W., & Walker, W. (Eds.). (2013). *Public Policy Analysis: New Developments*. London: Springer.

van Nispen, F., & de Jong, M. (2017). Evidence-Based Budgetary Policy: Speaking Truth to Power? In M. Brans, I. Geva-May, & M. Howlett (Eds.), *Routledge Handbook of Comparative Policy Analysis* (pp. 143–165). London: Routledge.

Veselý, A. (2017). Policy Analysis in the Central Government. In M. Brans, I. Geva-May, & M. Howlett (Eds.), *Routledge Handbook of Comparative Policy Analysis* (pp. 103–117). London: Routledge.

Vining, A., & Boardman, A. (2017). Business Associations and the Public Policy Process: When Do they Do Policy Analysis? In M. Brans, I. Geva-May, & M. Howlett (Eds.), *Routledge Handbook of Comparative Policy Analysis* (pp. 261–275). London: Routledge.

Vining, A., & Weimer, D. (2010). Policy Analysis. *PAR Foundations of Public Administration*. Retrieved from http://faculty.cbpp.uaa.alaska.edu/afgjp/PADM601%20Fall%202012/Policy%20Analysis.pdf.

Walker, W., Marchau, V., & Kwakkel, J. (2013). Uncertainty in the Framework of Policy Analysis. In W. Thissen & W. Walker (Eds.), *Public Policy Analysis: New Developments* (pp. 215–262). London: Springer.

Walker, W., & van Daalen, C. E. (2013). System Models for Policy Analysis. In W. Thissen & W. Walker (Eds.), *Public Policy Analysis: New Developments* (pp. 157–184). London: Springer.

Wolfs, W., & De Winter, L. (2017). Policy Analysis in the Legislative Branch. In M. Brans, I. Geva-May, & M. Howlett (Eds.), *Routledge Handbook of Comparative Policy Analysis* (pp. 199–212). London: Routledge.

CHAPTER 4

What Insights from Policy Process Research Do Policy Analysts Need to Know?

Abstract This chapter describes insights from policymaking studies, suggesting how they might be incorporated in policy analysis guides. Key factors include the psychology of policymaking and the main components of complex policymaking environments. This chapter outlines a collection of theories of the policy process and explains their implications for policy analysis.

Keywords Policy analysis • Policy process theories • Policymaking psychology • Policymaking environments • The new policy sciences

INTRODUCTION

Policy studies often begin by comparing two ideal-types with two stories of policymaking in the real world (Cairney 2020). First, policymakers are 'comprehensively rational', which means that they can process all policy-relevant facts, combine their values with information to rank their preferences consistently, and anticipate fully the effects of their choices. Second, the policy process resembles a clearly defined and simple 'cycle', containing a linear set of stages, from identifying a problem and possible solutions, to implementing and evaluating chosen solutions.

Imagine writing policy analysis in this ideal-type world, in which there is a single powerful 'rational' policymaker at the heart of government, making policy via an orderly cycle. Your audience would be easy to identify at each stage, your analysis would be relatively simple, and you would not need to worry about what happens after you make a recommendation for policy change (since the selection of a solution would lead to implementation). You could adopt a simple five-step policy analysis method, use widely used tools such as cost-benefit analysis to compare solutions, and know where the results would feed into the policy process. Classic policy analysis texts do not make these assumptions, but they often seem to tap into this basic step-by-step idea, and focus more on the science and craft of policy analysis than the complex policymaking context in which it takes place.

In the real world, policymakers face 'bounded rationality', in which they only have the ability to pay attention to a tiny proportion of available facts, are unable to separate those facts from their values (since we use our beliefs to evaluate the meaning of facts), struggle to make clear and consistent choices, and do not know what impact they will have. They engage in a far messier and less predictable world in which no single 'centre' has the power to turn a recommendation into an outcome. To incorporate these insights fully is to alter profoundly the ways in which we think about the impact of policy analysis.

INCORPORATE POLICYMAKER PSYCHOLOGY INTO POLICY ANALYSIS

Cairney and Weible (2017: 623) argue that policy analysis texts acknowledge *one* main aspect of policymaker psychology: 'the exhortation to keep policy analysis short, minimise jargon, and favour concrete examples over an abstract problem, is based generally on the need to minimise the cognitive load on your audience'. Yet, most texts only scratch the surface of relevant psychological insights, in which people draw on cognition and emotion to make choices with limited information, and are subject to so-called cognitive biases such as:

- A vulnerability to the ways in which other people frame problems.
- To see vivid events as more representative of reality than they are, and therefore pay disproportionate attention to some issues.
- To sum up entire social groups with reference to very few, and therefore characterise target populations in a simplistic way.

- To value losses more than gains, and therefore misjudge trade-offs between current and future policy choices.
- To have unrealistic hopes for the things to which they have already committed, which can produce inertia or a status quo bias.
- To see patterns and possess a 'need for coherence', and therefore assign too much certainty to limited information.
- To converge towards 'groupthink', which can limit the range of options considered by governments.
- Policymaker anxiety can cause them to make rushes to judgement, and act quickly without full consideration of policy analysis (Cairney 2020: 60; Gigerenzer 2015; Kahneman 2012; Cairney and Kwiatkowski 2017).

Cairney (2020: 233) summarises the ways in which policy theories identify a wide range of implications of policymaker psychology in relation to different aspects of policy processes, including:

1. *Limited attention, and lurches of attention.* Policymakers can only pay attention to a tiny proportion of their responsibilities, and policymaking organisations struggle to process all policy-relevant information. They prioritise some issues and information and ignore the rest (Baumgartner and Jones 2009, 2015).
2. *Power and ideas.* Some ways of understanding and describing the world dominate policy debate, helping some actors and marginalising others.
3. *Beliefs and coalitions.* Policy actors see the world through the lens of their beliefs. They engage in politics to turn their beliefs into policy, form coalitions with people who share them, and compete with coalitions who don't (Sabatier and Weible 2007).
4. *Dealing efficiently with complexity.* Actors engage in 'trial-and-error strategies' or use their 'social tribal instincts' to rely on 'different decision heuristics to deal with uncertain and dynamic environments' (Cairney 2013: 279; Lubell 2013: 544).
5. *Framing and narratives.* Policy audiences are vulnerable to manipulation when they rely on other actors to help them understand the world. Actors tell simple stories to persuade their audience to see a policy problem and its solution in a particular way (Crow and Jones 2018).

6. *The social construction of populations.* Policymakers draw on quick emotional judgements, and social stereotypes, to propose benefits to some target populations and punishments for others (Schneider and Ingram 1997, 2005).
7. *Rules and norms.* Institutions are the formal rules but also the informal understandings that 'exist in the minds of the participants and sometimes are shared as implicit knowledge rather than in an explicit and written form' (Ostrom 2007: 23). They represent a way to narrow information searches efficiently to make choices quickly.
8. *Learning.* Policy learning is a political process in which actors engage selectively with information, not a rational search for truth. Dunlop and Radaelli (2013, 2018) show that only one of the key ways to learn is from experts/analysts to policymakers (*epistemic* learning), while others include *bargaining* (producing new knowledge about strategies to win), *reflective* (combining insights from many sources through deliberation), and *hierarchy* (generating knowledge on central control or local discretion).

These insights provide a wide range of possibilities for policy analysts to learn about the likely impact of their analysis. *To some extent*, we can find elements of psychology in policy analysis strategy, such as when advice on framing problems describes it as a highly political exercise with potential winners and losers. However, when compared to Bacchi (2009) and Stone (2012) in the next chapter, we find in classic texts a relative tendency to identify the technical aspects of framing, and the techniques that analysts can use to avoid misrepresenting a problem. Rather, policymaker psychology is about the ways in which people combine cognition and emotion to process policy analysis, which opens up far more possibilities and the need for additional techniques. For example:

> consider if policymakers feel antagonism towards a person giving what they perceive to be dubious evidence without realising they are 'carrying' a group emotion with them ... A sole focus on cognitive load is futile if policymakers have a reason to not pay attention to an issue *at all* or to *reject the analysis completely* because they find it threatening. (Cairney and Weible 2017: 623)

Further, 'if people engage emotionally with information, there is no way to appeal to all audiences with the same information' (2017: 623). Rather, the choice may be to tailor your analysis to a policymaker's beliefs and emotions or accept that your analysis may go unread. In other words, we cannot simply make an 'evidence-based' case for identifying and solving a policy problem. Theory-informed policy analysis is about 'skilful persuasion which appeals to emotion', and policy theories provide extensive discussion about how policy actors seek to persuade with evidence. For example, Cairney et al. (2016: 401) identify examples from the literature, including:

- 'Combine facts with emotional appeals to prompt lurches of policy maker attention from one policy image to another (True et al. 2007, 161).

- Tell simple stories that are easy to understand, help manipulate people's biases, apportion praise and blame, and highlight the moral and political value of solutions (Jones et al. 2014).

- Interpret new evidence through the lens of the pre-existing beliefs of actors within coalitions, some of which dominate policy networks (Weible et al. 2012)

- Produce a policy solution that is feasible and exploit a time when policymakers have the opportunity to adopt it. (Kingdon 1984)'

INCORPORATE POLICY CONTEXT AND COMPLEXITY

If policy analysis takes place in a complex policymaking system, we need to account for our lack of understanding of the policymaking context when researching and providing advice (compare with Bardach and Patashnik 2020: 64–5 on the 'emergent-features' problem). There are many policy theories and concepts devoted to the identification of a wider environment in which policymaking takes place. Each concept reinforces the point that policymakers do not operate in a world in which they can oversee a policy cycle with linear stages. Policy analysis texts recognise these constraints *to some extent*, but seek primarily to deal with them by taking practical steps to reduce complexity for a client. A wider perspective requires us to draw more from policy theories.

For this reason alone, I recommend not thinking of the policy cycle when you imagine the policy process. However, this act is difficult without replacing it with other images. Therefore, for example, consider Fig. 4.1 in which there is an almost overwhelming (in effect, infinite) amount of 'cycles', of different size and shape, taking place at the same time, to the extent that the image no longer gives us any guidance on what happens. It exists simply to reject simplicity.

Then, for the sake of simple exposition, consider Fig. 4.2, which describes policymaker psychology within a policymaking environment that can be summed up in five or six concepts (Heikkila and Cairney 2017; Cairney 2020: 101–2).

1. *Actors.* The environment contains many policymakers and influencers spread across many levels and types of government (let us call the latter 'venues' in which authoritative choice takes place). Consequently, it is not a straightforward task to identify and know your audience, particularly if the problem you seek to solve requires a combination of policy instruments controlled by different actors.
2. *Institutions.* Each venue contains 'institutions', or collection of practices driven by formal and informal rules. Formal rules are often written down or known widely. Informal rules are the unwritten rules, norms, and practices that are difficult to understand, and may not even be understood in the same way by participants. They may exist only 'in the minds of participants' (Ostrom 2007: 23) and perhaps followed 'out of awareness' or without conscious thought (Cairney and Kwiatkowski 2017: 3). Consequently, it is difficult to know if your solution will be a good fit with the standard operating procedures of organisations, and therefore if it is politically feasible or too challenging.
3. *Networks.* Policymakers and influencers operate in subsystems (in other words, specialist parts of political systems). They form networks or coalitions built on the exchange of resources or facilitated by trust underpinned by shared beliefs or previous cooperation. Effective policy analysis may require you to engage with or become part of such networks, to allow you to understand the unwritten 'rules of the game' and encourage your audience to trust the messenger. In some cases, the rules relate to your willingness to accept current losses for future gains, such as to accept the limited impact of your analysis now in the hope of acceptance at the next opportunity.
4. *Ideas.* Political actors relate their analysis to shared understandings of the world—how it is, and how it should be—which are often so

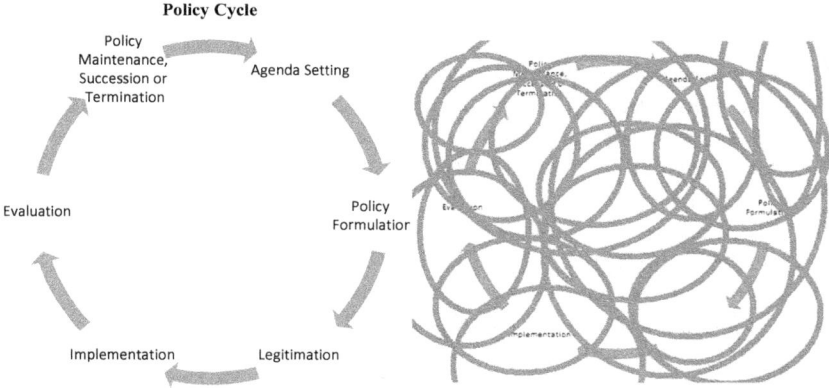

Fig. 4.1 The policy cycle versus infinite cycles. (Source: Cairney 2017)

Fig. 4.2 An image of the policy process. (Source: Cairney 2017)

established as to be taken for granted. Common terms include paradigms, hegemons, core beliefs, and monopolies of understandings. These dominant frames of reference give meaning to your policy solution. They prompt you to couch your solutions in terms of, for example, a strong attachment to evidence-based cases in public health, value for money in treasury departments, or with regard to core principles such as liberalism or socialism in different political systems.
5. *Context and events.* Your solutions relate to socioeconomic context and events which can be impossible to ignore and out of the control of policymakers. Such factors range from a political system's geography, demography, social attitudes, economy, while events can be routine elections on unexpected crises. To some extent, crises can be described opportunistically to encourage new solutions. Or, the unpredictability of events can prompt you to be modest in your claims, since the environment may be more important to outcomes than your favoured intervention.

From Concepts to Theories: Key Approaches Relevant to Policy Analysis

Policy theories try to incorporate these factors into an overall conception of policy processes, and the following summaries of key examples help guide further discussions of policy analysis in Part II (they are drawn from my blog's 500 and 1000 word summaries—https://paulcairney.wordpress.com—and you can find fuller descriptions in Cairney 2020).

Narrative Policy Framework

The Narrative Policy Framework (NPF) identifies the narrative strategies of actors seeking to exploit other actors' cognitive biases. A narrative contains four elements:

- *Setting.* It relates to a policymaking context, including institutional and socioeconomic factors.
- *Characters.* It contains at least one actor, such as a hero or villain.
- *Plot.* Common story arcs include heroes going on a journey or facing and overcoming adversity, often relating to villains causing trouble and victims suffering tragedy.

- *Moral.* A story's take-home point describes the cause of, and solution to, the policy problem.

Studies of narrative suggest that these techniques have *some* impact (Jones 2014). Empirical NPF studies suggest that narrators are effective when they: use an audience's fundamental beliefs to influence their more malleable beliefs; tie their story to a hero rather than a villain; help the audience imagine a concrete, not abstract, problem; and connect individual stories to a well-understood 'grand narrative'. They also compete with others, using stories to 'socialise' or 'privatise' issues, romanticise their own coalition's aim while demonising others, or encourage governments to distribute benefits to heroic target populations and punishments to villains.

However, their success depends heavily on the context, and stories tend to be most influential on the audiences *predisposed to accept them* (Cairney 2020: 66–9). Particular narratives may only be influential during a time the audience is receptive, or when the story fits with the audience's beliefs. Still, a story could make the difference between thought and action, such as when people prioritise one problem at the expense of the rest. We may struggle to persuade people to change their beliefs, but we can encourage them to act by focusing their attention to one belief over another. People possess many contradictory beliefs, which suggests that (a) they could support many different goals or policy solutions and (b) their support may relate strongly to the context and rules that determine the order and manner in which they make choices. To encourage them to pay more attention to, and place more value on, one belief (or one way to understand a policy problem) at the expense of another could make a large difference to policy (Crow and Jones 2018; see also the next chapter discussing Stone and Riker).

Social Construction and Policy Design
Social construction and policy design (SCPD) describes two main ways in which policymaking is 'degenerative' (Schneider and Ingram 1997, 2005, 2019; Schneider et al. 2014). First, high-profile politics and electoral competition can cause alienation. Politicians assign praise or blame to groups of people and make value judgements about who should be rewarded or punished by government. They base them on stereotypes of 'target populations', by (a) exploiting the ways in which many people think about

groups, or (b) making emotional and superficial judgements, backed up with selective use of facts.

These judgements have a 'feed-forward' effect: they are reproduced in policies, practices, and institutions. Such 'policy designs' can endure for years or decades. The distribution of rewards and sanctions is cumulative and difficult to overcome. Policy design has an impact on citizens, who participate in politics according to how they are characterised by government. Many know they will be treated badly; their engagement will be dispiriting. Some groups have the power to challenge the way they are described by policymakers (and the media and public) and receive benefits behind the scenes despite their poor image. However, many people feel powerless, become disenchanted with politics, and do not engage in the democratic process.

Second, bureaucrats and experts can exacerbate problems of citizen exclusion when they process low salience issues out of the public spotlight. Policies dominated by bureaucratic interests often alienate citizens receiving services. Or a small elite dominates policymaking when there is high acceptance that (a) the best policy is 'evidence based' and (b) the evidence should come from experts. In both cases, policy design is not informed by routine citizen participation, and it *exacerbates* the profound forms of inequality that policymakers often claim to be solving (compare with 'Policy Analysis for Marginalised Groups' in Chap. 5).

Multiple Streams Analysis
In the artificial policy cycle world, 'comprehensively rational' policymakers combine their values with evidence to define policy problems and their aims, 'neutral' bureaucracies produce many possible solutions consistent with those aims, and policymakers select the 'best' or most 'evidence-based' solution, setting in motion a cycle of stages including legitimation, implementation, evaluation, and the choice to maintain or change policy. In the real world, policymaking is not so simple, and three 'stages' seem messed up (Kingdon 1984; Zahariadis 2003; Cairney and Jones 2016; Herweg et al. 2018):

- *Defining problems* ('problem stream'). There is too much going on in the world, and too much information about problems. So, policymakers have to ignore most problems and most ways to understand them. They use cognitive short cuts to help them pay attention to a manageable number of issues and address problems without fully understanding them. Problems get attention based on how they are framed: actors use evidence to reduce uncertainty and persuasion to reduce ambiguity (they focus our minds on one way to understand a problem).

- *Producing solutions* ('policy stream'). When policymaker attention lurches to a problem, it's too late to produce a new solution that is technically feasible (will it work as intended?) and politically feasible (is it acceptable to enough people in the 'community'?). While attention lurches quickly, feasible solutions take time to develop.
- *Making choices* ('politics stream'). The willingness and ability of policymakers to select a solution is fleeting, based on their beliefs, perception of the 'national mood', and the feedback they receive from interest groups and political parties.

Don't think of these things as linear 'stages'. Instead, they are independent 'streams' which sometimes come together during a brief 'window of opportunity'. All key factors—heightened attention to a problem (problem stream), an available and feasible solution (policy stream), and the motive to select it (politics stream)—must come together at the same time, or the opportunity for major policy change is lost. Think of a space launch in which policymakers will abort the mission unless every factor is just right (Cairney 2018).

Complex Systems Theory and Punctuated Equilibrium Theory
Complex systems approaches suggest that policymaking systems have the following broad properties:

1. A complex system is greater than the sum of its parts; actors interact with each other, share information, and combine to produce systemic behaviour.
2. Some attempts to influence complex systems are dampened (negative feedback) while others are amplified (positive feedback).
3. Systems are 'sensitive to initial conditions' that produce a long-term momentum or 'path dependence'.
4. They exhibit 'emergence' or behaviour that results from the interaction between elements at a local level rather than central direction.
5. They may contain 'strange attractors' or demonstrate extended regularities of behaviour which may be interrupted by short bursts of change (see Cairney 2012, 2020; Geyer and Cairney 2015).

Punctuated Equilibrium Theory (PET) tells a story of complex policy-making systems that are stable *and* dynamic. Most policymaking exhibits long periods of stability, but with the ever-present potential for sudden instability. Most policies stay the same for long periods, and some change very quickly and dramatically. The overall pattern of policy change includes a huge number of minor changes and a small number of major changes (Baumgartner et al. 2018).

We can explain this dynamic with reference to bounded rationality: since policymakers cannot consider all issues at all times, they ignore most and promote relatively few to the top of their agenda. This *lack of attention* to most issues helps explain why most policies may not change, while *intense periods of attention* to some issues prompt new ways to frame and solve policy problems. Some explanation comes from the power of participants, to (a) minimise attention and maintain an established framing, or (b) expand attention in the hope of attracting new audiences more sympathetic to new ways of thinking. Further explanation comes from the scale of conflict, which is too large to understand, let alone control (Koski and Workman 2018).

The original PET story combines insights from the study of agenda setting and policy networks to demonstrate stable relationships between interest groups and policymakers (Baumgartner and Jones 2009). They endure when participants have built up trust and agreement—about the nature of a policy problem and how to address it—and ensure that few other actors have a legitimate role or interest in the issue. They come under pressure when issues attract high policymaker attention, such as following a 'focusing event' (Birkland 1997, 2016) or a successful attempt by some groups to 'venue shop' (seek influential audiences in another policymaking venue). When an issue reaches the top of this wider political agenda it is processed in a different way: more participants become involved, and they generate more ways to look at (and seek to solve) the problem. The key focus is the competition to frame or define a policy problem. The successful definition of a policy problem as technical or humdrum ensures that issues are monopolised and considered quietly in one venue. The reframing of that issue as crucial to other institutions, or the big political issues of the day, ensures that it will be considered by many audiences and processed in more than one venue (see Schattschneider 1960).

The modern PET story is more about complex systems and attention (Jones and Baumgartner 2005; Baumgartner and Jones 2015). Its analysis of bounded rationality remains crucial, since PET measures the consequences of the limited attention of individuals and organisations (Baumgartner 2017: 72). However, note the much greater quantification of policy change across entire political systems (see the Comparative Agendas Project, CAP). PET shows how policy actors and organisations contribute to 'disproportionate information processing', in which attention to information fluctuates out of proportion to (a) the size of policy problems and (b) the information on problems available to policymakers (Workman et al. 2009). It also shows that the same basic distribution of policy change—'hyperincremental' in most cases, but huge in some—is present in every political system studied by the CAP. This distribution of policy change has profound implications for our expectations on the impact of policy and policy analysis (see, e.g. 'How Far Would You Go to Secure Impact from Your Analysis?' in Chap. 12).

Advocacy Coalition Framework
People engage in politics to turn their beliefs into policy. They form advocacy coalitions with people who share their beliefs, and compete with other coalitions (Sabatier and Jenkins-Smith 1993; Sabatier and Weible 2007; Jenkins-Smith et al. 2018; Weible and Ingold 2018). The action takes place within a subsystem devoted to a policy issue, and a wider policymaking process that provides constraints and opportunities to coalitions. The policy process contains multiple actors and levels of government. It displays a mixture of intensely politicised disputes and routine activity. There is much uncertainty about the nature and severity of policy problems. The full effects of policy may be unclear for over a decade. The advocacy coalition framework (ACF) sums it up in the *ACF flow diagram* (Fig. 4.3 overleaf).

Policy actors use their beliefs to understand, and seek influence in, this world. Beliefs about how to interpret the cause of and solution to policy problems, and the role of government in solving them, act as a glue to bind actors together within coalitions. Beliefs allow them to select and interpret policy-relevant information and decide who to trust. If the policy issue is technical and humdrum, there may be room for routine cooperation (Ingold and Gschwend 2014). If the issue is highly charged, then people romanticise their own cause and demonise their opponents (Sabatier et al. 1987). The outcome is often long-term policymaking stability and policy continuity because the 'core' beliefs of coalitions (and the 'relatively stable parameters' of political system) are unlikely to shift and one coalition may dominate the subsystem for long periods.

62 P. CAIRNEY

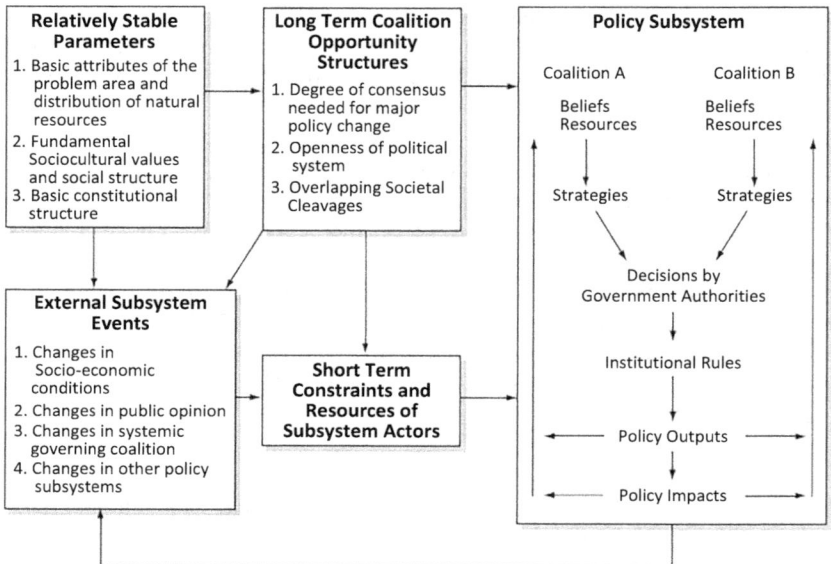

Fig. 4.3 The ACF flow diagram. (Source: Weible et al. 2016: 6)

There are two main sources of change. First, coalitions engage in policy-oriented learning to remain competitive and adapt to new information about policy. This process often produces minor change because coalitions learn on their own terms. They learn how to retain their coalition's strategic advantage and use the information they deem most relevant. Second, 'shocks' affect the positions of coalitions within subsystems. Shocks are the combination of events and coalition responses. External shocks are prompted by events outside the subsystem, including the election of a new government with different ideas, or the effect of socioeconomic change. Internal shocks are prompted by policy failure. Both may prompt major change as members of one coalition question their beliefs in the light of new evidence. Or, another coalition may adapt more readily to its new policy environment and exploit events to gain competitive advantage. In such cases, coalitions compete to improve their positions within subsystems using resources such as the ability to gather and interpret information, mobilise public support, secure funding for campaigns, and show skilful leadership. In that context, policy analysis is a political act that may take place within coalitions rather than across subsystems.

Institutional Analysis and Development Framework
The institutional analysis and development framework (IAD) provides a language, and way of thinking, about the ways in which different institutions foster collective action (Ostrom 2007, 2011). Most famously, Ostrom (1990) explains how to rethink 'tragedies of the commons' and encourage better management of 'common pool resources' (CPRs; see Heikkila and Carter 2017). Ostrom rejects the assumption that disastrous collective action problems (such as excessive deforestation, pollution, or diminished natural resources) are inevitable unless we 'privatise' CPRs or secure major government intervention. Rather, there is evidence that people often work collectively and effectively without major coercion. Self-governance, communal action, or cross-governmental cooperation often works (Schlager and Cox 2018: 216). People are social beings who share information, build trust by becoming known as reliable and predictable, and come together to produce, monitor, and enforce rules for the group's benefit. They produce agreements with each other that could be enforced if necessary.

The IAD helps us analyse these cooperative arrangements. For example, Ostrom (1990) describes eight 'design principles' of enduring and effective CPR management shared by many real-world examples, including: clear boundaries; tailord to local conditions; those affected by the rules should help shape them; CPR monitors are users or accountable to users; the penalties for rule-breaking are only high if the choice is part of a pattern or if rule-breaking would be catastrophic; and conflict resolution is frequent, rapid, and low cost. These design principles help explain why some communities manage CPRs successfully. They allow users to share the same commitment and expect the long-term benefits to be worthwhile.

However, Ostrom stresses that there is no blueprint—no hard and fast rules—to CPR management. There are three particular complications. First, design principles are important to developing trust and solidarity, but so are 'evolutionary' changes to behaviour. Actors have often learned about rule efficacy—to encourage cooperation and punish opportunism—through trial-and-error over a long period. Second, institutions contain a large, complicated set of rules that serve many different purposes, and need to be understood and analysed in different ways. Different purposes include: how many actors are part of an action situation, and the role they play; what they must/must not do; who is eligible to participate; the rewards or sanctions; and so on. Further, the rules about the other rules include: 'operational' rules on day-to-day issues; 'collective choice' rules about how to make those rules; 'constitutional' rules on who can decide those rules and who can monitor and enforce them; and 'metaconstitutional' analysis of how to design these constitutions with reference to the wider political and social context (Ostrom et al. 2014: 285).

The IAD language is also a feature of studies of 'polycentric' governance, in which many different 'centres' or sources of authoritative choice need to cooperate to produce policy (Aligica and Tarko 2012; Cairney et al. 2016). Additional literatures include 'institutional collective action' (Feiock 2013; Swann and Kim 2018) and the 'ecology of games' framework (Lubell 2013). Such approaches inform heavily our discussions of 'co-producing' policy analysis (see Chap. 8).

What Are the Implications of These Extra Considerations?

Much of the policymaking literature suggests that the context for policymaking may be more important than the actual substance of your policy advice. Cairney and Weible (2017: 624–5) draw on these insights to suggest how a policy analyst can be an effective messenger:

> focus on engagement for the long term to develop the resources necessary to maximise the impact of policy analysis and understand the context in which the information is used. Among the advantages of long-term engagement are learning the 'rules of the game' in organisations, forming networks built on trust and a track record of reliability, learning how to 'soften' policy solutions according to the beliefs of key policymakers and influencers, and spotting 'windows of opportunity' to bring together attention to a problem, a feasible solution, and the motive and opportunity of policymakers to select it … In short, the substance of your analysis only has meaning in relation to the context in which it is used. Further, generating trust in the messenger and knowing your audience may be more important to success than presenting the evidence. (Cairney and Weible 2017)

Further, the insights in this chapter help us generate a much wider range of implications for policy analysis. First, they reinforce and explain

Chap. 3, which states that policy analysis is no longer about a small group of analysts with a direct line to power. The policy cycle, built on such a simple understanding, does not help us identify key players, organisational or network rules, the role of dominant ideas, or the socioeconomic context. Instead, we have a snapshot of an artificially simple process that may not exist. Therefore, avoid the idea that the selection of a policy solution sets in motion an inevitable process of legitimation, implementation, and evaluation. Instead, your analysis may be multi-faceted, prompting you to track progress and make further recommendations (Dunn 2017).

Second, complexity theorists generate a lot of recommendations for policymakers and their advisors (e.g. Geyer 2012; summarised in Cairney 2020: 106–7). They include the following suggestions: (a) law-like behaviour is difficult to identify; so a policy that was successful in one context may not have the same effect in another; (b) policymaking systems are difficult to control, and policymakers should not be surprised when their interventions do not have the desired effect; (c) use trial-and-error rather than relying on a single policy strategy; and (d) give local actors the freedom to adapt quickly, rather than (d) seeking order, via rigid hierarchies and centrist policy strategies. In other words, analysts should avoid 'single-shot' policy analysis in which there is a one-size-fits-all policy solution. A policy that works here and now may not work there or later.

Third, encourage critical analysis among your audience. This may be the trickiest task of all. An emotionally or cognitively satisfying solution may be based on a simple description of a problem and the sense that it can be solved in a quite straightforward way. Yet, policy success may also depend on your audience recognising its need to learn continuously and adapt strategies through processes such as trial and error.

This general advice only scratches the surface of the implications for policy analysis. It focuses primarily on how to take pragmatic steps built on a wider awareness of the policymaking context. To make full use of policy theory insights, we also need to consider the wider political context in which people exercise power to get attention for their policy-relevant knowledge, and define problems and solutions, at the expense of others. Some policy analysis may focus on the win-win scenario, but the next chapter provides a collection of ways in which we can be sceptical about such a framing. It allows us to consider the incomplete ways in which analysts respond to political and policymaking contexts. When combined, these two chapters prompt us to explore a series of themes in which we go much further to identify power-based dilemmas for enlightened and theory-informed policy analysts (see, e.g. 'How Far Would You Go to Secure Impact from Your Analysis?' in Chap. 12).

References

Aligica, P., & Tarko, V. (2012). Polycentricity: From Polanyi to Ostrom, and Beyond. *Governance, 25*(2), 237–262.

Bacchi, C. (2009). *Analysing Policy: What's the Problem Represented to Be?* NSW: Pearson.

Bardach, E., & Patashnik, E. (2020). *A Practical Guide for Policy Analysis* (6th ed.) (International Student edition). London: Sage.

Baumgartner, F. (2017). Endogenous Disjoint Change. *Cognitive Systems Research, 44*, 69–73. https://doi.org/10.1016/j.cogsys.2017.04.001.

Baumgartner, F., & Jones, B. (2009). *Agendas and Instability in American Politics* (2nd ed.). Chicago: University of Chicago Press.

Baumgartner, F., & Jones, B. (2015). *The Politics of Information.* Chicago: University of Chicago Press.

Baumgartner, F., Jones, B., & Mortensen, P. (2018). Punctuated Equilibrium Theory. In C. Weible & P. Sabatier (Eds.), *Theories of the Policy Process* (4th ed.). Chicago: Westview.

Birkland, T. (1997). *After Disaster: Agenda Setting, Public Policy and Focusing Events.* Washington, DC: Georgetown University Press.

Birkland, T. (2016). Attention and Natural Disasters. In N. Zahariadis (Ed.), *Handbook of Public Policy Agenda-Setting.* Cheltenham: Edward Elgar.

Cairney, P. (2012). Complexity Theory in Political Science and Public Policy. *Political Studies Review, 10*(3), 346–358.

Cairney, P. (2013). What Is Evolutionary Theory and How Does It Inform Policy Studies? *Policy and Politics, 41*(2), 279–298.

Cairney, P. (2017). 5 Images of the Policy Process. *Paul Cairney: Politics & Public Policy.* Retrieved from https://paulcairney.wordpress.com/2017/07/10/5-images-of-the-policy-process/.

Cairney, P. (2018). Three Habits of Successful Policy Entrepreneurs. *Policy and Politics, 46*(2), 199–217.

Cairney, P. (2020). *Understanding Public Policy* (2nd ed.). London: Red Globe.

Cairney, P., Heikkila, T., & Wood, M. (2019). *Making Policy in a Complex World.* Cambridge: Cambridge University Press.

Cairney, P., & Jones, M. (2016). Kingdon's Multiple Streams Approach: What Is the Empirical Impact of this Universal Theory? *Policy Studies Journal, 44*(1), 37–58.

Cairney, P., & Kwiatkowski, R. (2017). How to Communicate Effectively with Policymakers: Combine Insights from Psychology and Policy Studies. *Palgrave Communications, 3*, 37. Retrieved from https://www.nature.com/articles/s41599-017-0046-8.

Cairney, P., & Weible, C. (2017). The New Policy Sciences: Combining the Cognitive Science of Choice, Multiple Theories of Context, and Basic and Applied Analysis. *Policy Sciences, 50*(4), 619–627.

Cairney, P., Oliver, K., & Wellstead, A. (2016). To Bridge the Divide between Evidence and Policy: Reduce Ambiguity as Much as Uncertainty. *Public Administration Review, 76*(3), 399–402.

Crow, D., & Jones, M. (2018). Narratives as Tools for Influencing Policy Change. *Policy & Politics, 46*(2), 217–234.

Dunlop, C., & Radaelli, C. (2013). Systematising Policy Learning: From Monolith to Dimensions. *Political Studies Review, 61*(3), 599–619.

Dunlop, C., & Radaelli, C. (2018). The Lessons of Policy Learning: Types, Triggers, Hindrances and Pathologies. *Policy & Politics, 46*(2), 255–272.

Dunn, W. (2017). *Public Policy Analysis* (6th ed.). Routledge.

Feiock, R. (2013). The Institutional Collective Action Framework. *Policy Studies Journal, 41*(3), 397–425.

Geyer, R. (2012). Can Complexity Move UK Policy beyond 'Evidence-Based Policy Making' and the 'Audit Culture'? *Political Studies, 60*(1), 20–43.

Geyer, R., & Cairney, P. (Eds.). (2015). *Handbook on Complexity and Public Policy*. Cheltenham: Edward Elgar.

Gigerenzer, G. (2015). *Risk Savvy*. London: Penguin.

Heikkila, T., & Carter, D. (2017). Common Pool Resources. *Oxford Bibliographies*. https://doi.org/10.1093/OBO/9780199363445-0011.

Herweg, N., Zahariadis, N., & Zohlnhöfer, R. (2018). The Multiple Streams Framework: Foundations, Refinements, and Empirical Applications. In C. Weible & P. Sabatier (Eds.), *Theories of the Policy Process* (4th ed.). Chicago, IL: Westview Press.

Ingold, K., & Gschwend, M. (2014). Science in Policy-Making: Neutral Experts or Strategic Policy-Makers? *West European Politics, 37*(5), 993–1018.

Jenkins-Smith, H., Nohrstedt, D., Weible, C., & Ingold, K. (2018). The Advocacy Coalition Framework: An Overview of the Research Program. In C. Weible & P. Sabatier (Eds.), *Theories of the Policy Process* (pp. 145–182). London: Routledge.

Jones, M. (2014). Communicating Climate Change: Are Stories Better than 'Just the Facts. *Policy Studies Journal, 42*(4), 644–673.

Jones, B., & Baumgartner, F. (2005). *The Politics of Attention*. Chicago, IL: University of Chicago Press.

Jones, M., Shanahan, E., & McBeth, M. (Eds.). (2014). *The Science of Stories: Applications of the Narrative Policy Framework in Public Policy Analysis*. New York, NY: Palgrave Macmillan.

Kahneman, D. (2012). *Thinking Fast and Slow*. London: Penguin.

Kingdon, J. (1984). *Agendas, Alternatives and Public Policies*. New York, NY: Harper Collins.

Koski, C., & Workman, S. (2018). Drawing Practical Lessons from Punctuated Equilibrium Theory. *Policy and Politics, 46*(2), 293–308.

Lubell, M. (2013). Governing Institutional Complexity: The Ecology of Games Framework. *Policy Studies Journal, 41*(3), 537–559.

Ostrom, E. (1990). *Governing the Commons: The Evolution of Institutions for Collective Action*. Cambridge: Cambridge University Press.

Ostrom, E. (2007). Institutional Rational Choice. In P. Sabatier (Ed.), *Theories of the Policy Process* (2nd ed.). Cambridge, MA: Westview Press.

Ostrom, E. (2011). Background on the Institutional Analysis and Development Framework. *Policy Studies Journal, 39*(1), 7–27.

Ostrom, E., Cox, M., & Schlager, E. (2014). An Assessment of the Institutional Analysis and Development Framework and Introduction of the Social-Ecological Systems Framework. In P. Sabatier & C. Weible (Eds.), *Theories of the Policy Process* (3rd ed.). Boulder, CO: Westview Press.

Sabatier, P., Hunter, S., & McLaughlin, S. (1987). The Devil Shift: Perceptions and Misperceptions of Opponents. *The Western Political Quarterly, 40*(3), 449–476.

Sabatier, P., & Jenkins-Smith, H. (Eds.). (1993). *Policy Change and Learning: An Advocacy Coalition Approach*. Boulder, CO: Westview Press.

Sabatier, P., & Weible, C. (2007). The Advocacy Coalition Framework: Innovations and Clarifications. In P. Sabatier (Ed.), *Theories of the Policy Process*. Boulder, CO: Westview Press.

Schattschneider, E. E. (1960). *The Semi-sovereign People*. Fort Worth, TX: Harcourt Brace, 1975 edition.

Schlager, E., & Cox, M. (2018). The IAD Framework and the SES Framework. In C. Weible & P. Sabatier (Eds.), *Theories of the Policy Process* (4th ed.). Chicago: Westview Press.

Schneider, A., & Ingram, H. (1997). *Policy Design for Democracy*. Kansas: University of Kansas Press.

Schneider, A., & Ingram, H. (Eds.). (2005). *Deserving and Entitled: Social Construction and Public Policy*. Albany: State University of New York Press.

Schneider, A., & Ingram, H. (2019). Social Constructions, Anticipatory Feedback Strategies, and Deceptive Public Policy. *Policy Studies Journal, 47*(2), 206–236.

Schneider, A., Ingram, H., & deLeon, P. (2014). Democratic Policy Design: Social Construction of Target Populations. In P. Sabatier & C. Weible (Eds.), *Theories of the Policy Process*. Boulder: Westview Press.

Stone, D. (2012). *Policy Paradox: The Art of Political Decision Making* (3rd ed.). London: Norton.

Swann, W., & Kim, S. (2018). Practical Prescriptions for Governing Fragmented Governments. *Policy and Politics, 46*(2), 273–292.

True, J., Jones, B., & Baumgartner, F. (2007). Punctuated Equilibrium Theory. In P. Sabatier (Ed.), *Theories of the Policy Process* (2nd ed.). Cambridge, MA: Westview Press.

Weible, C., Heikkila, T., deLeon, P., & Sabatier, P. (2012). Understanding and Influencing the Policy Process. *Policy Sciences, 45*(1), 1–21.

Weible, C., Heikkila, T., Ingold, K., & Fischer, M. (2016). Introduction. In C. Weible, T. Heikkila, K. Ingold, & M. Fischer (Eds.), *Policy Debates on Hydraulic Fracturing*. London: Palgrave Macmillan.

Weible, C., & Ingold, K. (2018). Why Advocacy Coalitions Matter and Practical Insights About Them. *Policy & Politics, 46*(2), 325–343.

Workman, S., Jones, B., & Jochim, A. (2009). Information Processing and Policy Dynamics. *Policy Studies Journal, 37*(1), 75–92.

Zahariadis, N. (2003). *Ambiguity and Choice in Public Policy*. Washington, DC: Georgetown University Press.

CHAPTER 5

What Insights from Wider Studies of Power, Knowledge, Politics, and Policy Do Policy Analysts Need to Consider?

Abstract This chapter shows how policy analysts can incorporate insights from wider studies of politics, with a particular emphasis on power, feminism, race, and decolonisation. It allows analysts to think about the meaning of policy analysis: what is it for, and who is it for? It also prompts us to reflect further on how we decide whose knowledge counts as high quality and policy relevant. As such, this discussion is as an antidote to too-simple descriptions of policy analysis as a five-step process to serve clients. Its alternative is to reflect on the concepts and approaches that help us interrogate whose policy-relevant knowledge counts, and should count.

Keywords Policy paradox • 'What's the problem represented to be?' • Decolonisation • Marginalised groups • Power and knowledge

INTRODUCTION

This chapter shows how policy analysts can incorporate insights from wider studies of politics, with a particular emphasis on power, feminism, race, and decolonisation. It allows analysts to think about the meaning of policy analysis: what is it for, and who is it for? It also prompts us to reflect further on how we decide whose knowledge counts as high quality and policy relevant.

As such, this discussion is as an antidote to too-simple descriptions of policy analysis as a five-step process to serve clients. If we describe policy analysis as a largely technical process, we are also exercising power to downplay the politics of knowledge production and use. If we describe it positively as a pragmatic process, we are downplaying the need to challenge inequalities of power associated with the status quo. This section's alternative is to reflect on the concepts and approaches that help us interrogate whose policy-relevant knowledge counts, and should count.

This chapter begins with two exemplars of approaches (Bacchi 2009; Stone 2012) that critique current studies of policy analysis directly. Both reject the idea that policy analysis can be a 'rational' or technical process to define problems and identify solutions. Rather, people exercise power to tell stories that benefit some and punish others. It then explores the ways in which we can build on these critiques with reference to a far wider literature with (generally) no direct focus on policy analysis texts. In particular, it describes the role of 'decolonising' knowledge, using Smith's (2012) work as an exemplar, reinforced by other classics in this field. It then explores how policy analysis critiques connect to studies that (a) identify inequalities in relation to race and gender and (b) challenge scholars and practitioners to pay more attention to inequalities in research and practice (Doucet 2019; Michener 2019). Overall, we find that treating policy analysis as pragmatic client-oriented activity misses the bigger picture in which analysts may contribute to the inequalities they study.

The Policy Paradox

Stone (2012: 379-85) rejects the image of policy analysis as a 'rationalist' project, driven by scientific and technical rules, and separable from politics. First, problem definition is not amenable to such simple analysis. The 'paradox' is that it is possible to define the same policies in contradictory ways; they can be 'two different things at once' (Stone 2012: 2). This paradox does not refer simply to a competition between *different actors* to define policy problems. Rather, the *same actor* can entertain very different ways to understand problems, and can juggle many criteria to decide that a policy outcome was a success and a failure (2012: 3; see also McConnell 2010). Or, the *same population* can report contradictory views—to support a specific policy response *and its complete opposite*—when asked different questions in the same poll (Stone 2012: 4). Therefore, second, *every policy analyst's choice is a political choice*, to define a problem and solution in one way and not another, and to categorise people and behaviour, backed by strategic persuasion and storytelling.

Five-step policy analysis may help clarify some of these political choices. However, it 'ignores our emotional feelings and moral intuitions' and the consequence of making choices in a 'polis' containing social actors rather than a 'market' containing individuals (Stone 2012: 11). Stone (2012: 10–11) rejects the over-reliance, in policy analysis, on the misleading claim that economic models can sum up political life, and that cost-benefit analyses can reduce a complex problem into the sum of individual preferences using a single unambiguous measure. Rather, many factors undermine such simplicity:

1. *People find it difficult to act 'rationally'.* They struggle to rank-order their preferences in a straightforward manner according to their values and self-interest. Instead, they maintain a contradictory mix of objectives, which can change according to context and their way of thinking—combining cognition and emotion—when processing information (2012: 12; 30–4; Cairney and Kwiatkowski 2017).
2. *People are social actors in a community.* Politics is characterised by 'a model of community where individuals live in a dense web of relationships, dependencies, and loyalties' and exercise power with reference to their beliefs as much as material interests (Stone 2012: 10; 20–36; compare with Ostrom 1990, 2011; Lubell 2013).
3. *Morals and emotions matter.* If people juggle contradictory aims and measures of success, then a story infused with 'metaphor and analogy', and appealing to values and emotions, prompts people 'to see a situation as one thing rather than another' and therefore draw attention to one aim at the expense of the others (Stone 2012: 11).
4. *Values and goals are ambiguous*: 'behind every policy issue lurks a contest over conflicting, though equally plausible, conceptions of the same abstract goal or value' (2012: 14). Examples of competing interpretations of valence issues include definitions of:

    - *Equity* debates focus on many questions. Which groups should be included? How do we assess merit? Should we identify key social groups, and rank populations within social groups, according to 'need'? How do we account for different people placing different values on a good or service? Which method of distribution (competition, lottery, election) should we use? How do we balance

individual, communal, and state-based interventions (2012: 39–62).
- *Efficiency,* to use the least resources to produce the same objective. Who determines the main goal, and how to balance multiple objectives? Who benefits from such actions? How do we define resources when balancing equity and efficiency: for example, does a public sector job and a social security payment represent a sunk cost to the state or a social investment in people (2012: 63–84)?
- *Welfare or Need,* according to factors including (a) the material versus symbolic value of goods, (b) short-term support versus a long-term investment in people, (c) measures of absolute poverty or relative inequality, and (d) debates on 'moral hazard' or the effect of social security on individual motivation (2012: 85–106).
- *Liberty,* according to (a) a general balancing of *freedom from coercion* and *freedom from the harm caused by others,* (b) debates on individual and state responsibilities, and (c) decisions on whose behaviour to change to reduce harm to what populations (2012: 107–28).
- *Security,* according to (a) our limited ability to measure risk scientifically, (b) *perceptions* of threat and *experiences* of harm, (c) debates on how much risk to safety to tolerate before intervening, (d) who to target and imprison, and (e) the effect of surveillance on perceptions of democracy (2012: 129–53).

In that context, policy analysis involves political actors using policy-relevant stories to influence the ways in which their audience understands the nature of policy problems and feasibility of solutions, within a wider context of policymaking in which people contest the proper balance between state, community, and market action. Stories influence multiple aspects of collective action. They *define interests and mobilise actors,* by framing issues with reference to an imagined social group and its competition (such as the people versus the elite, or strivers versus skivers) (2012: 229–47). They *obfuscate decisions,* by deliberately framing issues ambiguously, shifting goals, keeping feasible solutions off the agenda, and manipulating analyses to make their preferred solution seem the most efficient and popular. They *define the role and intended impact of policies,* such as when balancing punishments versus incentives to change behaviour, or individual versus collective behaviour (2012: 271–88). They *set and enforce rules* in a complex policymaking system where there are too many rules to enforce; a powerful narrative can draw attention to the need to enforce some rules at the expense of others (2012: 289–310). They *define human and legal rights,* when there are multiple, ambiguous, and intersecting rights, and the resources for the enforcement of some come at the expense of others (2012: 331–53). They *influence debate on the powers of each potential policymaking venue* in relation to factors including (a) the legitimate role of the state in market, community, family, and individual life, (b) how to select leaders, (c) the distribution of power between levels and types of government, and who to hold to account for policy outcomes (2012: 354–77).

In each case, a story is an act of persuasion, drawing on reason, facts, and indoctrination. Stone (2012: 311–30) highlights the context in which actors construct stories to persuade: people engage emotionally with information, people take certain situations for granted even though they produce unequal outcomes, facts are socially constructed, and there is unequal access to resources to gather and disseminate evidence (see also Schneider and Ingram 2005; Jones et al. 2014; Thibodeau and Boroditsky 2011). Key elements of storytelling include:

1. *Symbols,* which sum up an issue or an action in a single picture or word (2012: 157–8)
2. *Characters,* such as heroes or villain, who symbolise the cause of a problem or source of solution (2012: 159)
3. *Narrative arcs,* such as a battle by your hero to overcome adversity (2012: 160–8)
4. *Synecdoche,* to highlight one example of an alleged problem or social group to sum up its whole (2012: 168–71)
5. *Metaphor,* to create an association between a problem and something relatable, such as a virus or disease, a natural occurrence (such as an earthquake), something broken, something about to burst if overburdened, or war (2012: 171–78)
6. *Ambiguity,* to give people different reasons to support the same thing (2012: 178–82)
7. *Using numbers* to: categorise people and practices, select the measures to use, interpret the figures to evaluate or predict the results, project the sense that complex problems can be reduced to numbers, and assign authority to the counters (2012: 183–205)
8. *Assigning causation,* in relation to categories including accidental or natural, 'mechanical' or automatic (or in relation to institutions or

systems), and human-guided causes that have intended or unintended consequences (such as malicious intent versus recklessness). 'Causal strategies' include to: emphasise a natural versus human cause, relate it to 'bad apples' rather than systemic failure, and suggest that the problem was too complex to anticipate or influence. Actors use these arguments to influence rules, assign blame, identify 'fixers', and generate alliances among victims or potential supporters of change (2012: 206–28).

From Stories to Manipulation
Stone's focus on stories connects in important ways to Riker's (1986: ix) term 'heresthetic' to describe 'structuring the world so you can win'. People 'win politically because they have set up the situation in such a way that other people will want to join them'. They design the rules regarding how people make choices, such as to determine the order of choice because many policy preferences are 'intransitive' (if A is preferred to B and B to C, A is not necessarily preferred to C). They also exploit the ways in which people deal with 'bounded rationality', with cognitive shortcuts, to process information efficiently rather than comprehensively. Riker highlights the potential value of some combination of the following strategies:

- Make your preferred problem framing or solution as easy to understand as possible.
- Make other problems/solutions difficult to process, such as by presenting them in the abstract and providing excessive detail.
- Emphasise the high cognitive cost to the examination of all other options.
- Design the comparison of a small number of options to make sure that yours is the most competitive.
- Design the framing of choice. For example, is a vote primarily about the substantial issue or confidence in its proponents?
- Design the selection of criteria to evaluate options.
- Conspire to make sure that the proponent of your preferred choice is seen as heroic (and the proponent of another choice as of flawed character and intellect).
- Ensure that people make or vote for choices quickly, to ward off the possibility of further analysis and risk of losing control of the design of choice.

- Make sure that you engage in these strategies without being detected or punished.

These practices highlight the wider agenda setting context that analysts face when presenting evidence, values, and options. It is a truism in policy studies that the evidence does not speak for itself. Instead, people engage in effective communication and persuasion to assign meaning to the evidence. Further, it would be a mistake to expect success primarily from a well-written and argued policy analysis document. Rather, much of its fate depends on exploiting the procedures and rules that influence how people make choices.

The 'What's the Problem Represented to Be?' Approach

Bacchi (2009) uses this emphasis on the power of stories, and manipulation, to prompt us to think about the task of policy analysis in a wider political context. What's the problem represented to be (WPR) contrasts with models that take the nature of a policy problem for granted, seeking solutions on that basis. Bacchi's (2009: 30–1) key distinction is between 'problem' and 'problematisation'. Using the word 'problem' may imply that the nature of an issue is 'fixed and identifiable', 'self-evident', well-understood, agreed, or taken for granted. In contrast, 'problematisation' describes the ways in which people *create* policy problems as they make sense of them. Problem definition is a political process to identify how to define and address the social world, not a technical process built on a uniform understanding of its nature.

Bacchi (2009: xii; 1–24) presents a six-step process to understand problem definition:

1. "*What's the 'problem' represented to be in a specific policy?*" Problem definition can relate to: its alleged cause (such as the lifestyle of certain populations), how far a government should go to address it (such as to regulate, fund, or exhort), and which part of government is responsible (if it is, say, a problem of public health, social security, or criminal justice).
2. "*What presuppositions or assumptions underlie this representation of the 'problem'?*" WPR focuses on the 'deep-seated cultural values' that are taken for granted even though they underpin debate. Examples include the rules that political actors use to categorise 'target

populations', distinguish between normal or good versus deviant or punishable behaviour, and establish the role of government in 'private' or 'family' life (see also Schneider and Ingram 1997, 2005; Cairney 2019).

3. "*How has this representation of the 'problem' come about?*" Issues may be apparent for long periods before becoming problems for governments to solve. Explanations for intervention can include shifts in social attitudes or attention, changes in government, new information, and new technologies (such as in medicine, transport, or communication) that change social behaviour or make new interventions possible (see also Hogwood 1987). Further, old ways of solving problems can endure long after the problem seems to have changed (as can 'institutions'—see Streeck and Thelen 2005).

4. "*What is left unproblematic in this problem representation? Where are the silences? Can the 'problem' be thought about differently?*" Note the power to decide who—or what—is a problem, and the powerlessness of many people to challenge that choice. A population's 'problems' could be caused by their lifestyle *or the ways in which we interpret their behaviour.* The cause of traffic congestion could be over-reliance on cars or the absence of good infrastructure. Comparing problem definitions and cultural reference points, in different countries, can help identify which frames dominate.

5. "*What effects are produced by this representation of the 'problem'?*" Problem definitions can help close off debate. They help alienate and stigmatise some populations. They produce positive or negative material consequences and intended or unintended effects. Question 5 helps us ask who benefits from the current definition, and who might benefit from a new representation of the problem.

6. "*How/where has this representation of the 'problem' been produced, disseminated, and defended? How could it be questioned, disrupted, and replaced?*" People exercise power to create or defend these ways to characterise problems, in a context in which certain practices and ideas dominate debate. Bacchi argues that researchers have a responsibility to question them, and their 'origins, purposes, and effects', rather than 'buy into' them as a natural starting point for policy analysis. In other words, she challenges the assumption that policy analysis should simply be client-oriented.

Researching the policymaking context in this way raises a series of profound issues about policy and policy analysis, including the: rising use of statistics and data as a function of state surveillance, and the ways in which the state helps enforce norms about acceptable or deviant behaviour. This is a 'critical policy analysis' perspective with an in-built emancipatory function. The role of policy analysts is explicitly political, based on the assumption that policy benefits some groups and harms others, and hence the need to take 'the side of those who are harmed' (Bacchi 2009: 44). It rejects the idea that policy analysis exists simply to reduce uncertainty with the supply of evidence. Rather, policy actors exercise power to frame issues, reduce ambiguity, and determine the demand for evidence (see also Cairney et al. 2016).

WPR highlights the relationship between (a) our knowledge of the policy process and (b) the ways in which we use that knowledge to pursue a policy analysis strategy. Policy analysis is deliberately short and incomplete, often with a focus on what to exclude from discussion. It requires us to consider (a) our audience, (b) what to present and withhold, (c) how 'manipulative' to be, and (d) where to draw a notional line between providing evidence and advice, all within this wider political context (see Chap. 9).

Policy Analysis as Colonisation

These insights from Stone and Bacchi highlight wider concerns about the relationship between power, knowledge, and political analysis, summed up by Smith (2012: 10) as follows:

> Whose research is it? Who owns it? Whose interests does it serve? Who will benefit from it? Who has designed its questions and framed its scope? Who will carry it out? Who will write it up? How will its results be disseminated?

In particular, Smith (2012) identifies the profound impact of colonisation on the power to socially construct populations and assign government benefits and burdens, such as by equating 'indigenous' with 'dirtiness, savagery, rebellion and, since 9/11, terrorism' (2012: xi–xii). Further, academic and policy analytical research 'is inextricably linked to European imperialism and colonialism' (2012: 1; 21–6). Western research practices (and the European 'Enlightenment') reflect and reinforce political practices associated with colonial rule (2012: 2; 23).

People in indigenous communities describe researchers who exploit 'their culture, their knowledge, their resources' (and, in some cases, their bodies) to bolster their own career (2012: xi; 91–4; 102–7), in the context of a long history of subjugation and slavery that makes such practices possible (2012: 21–6; 28–9; 176–7) and 'justified as being for "the good of mankind"' (2012: 26). Western researchers think—hubristically—that they can produce a general understanding of the practices and cultures of indigenous peoples. Instead, they produce—irresponsibly or maliciously— negative and often dehumanising images that feed into policies 'employed to deny the validity of indigenous peoples' claim to existence' and solve the 'indigenous problem' (2012: 1; 8–9; 26–9; 62–5; 71–2; 81–91; 94–6). For example, research contributes to a tendency for governments to:

- identify, within indigenous communities, indicators of inequality in relation to factors such as health, education, crime, and family life
- relate inequalities to indigenous cultures and low intelligence
- dismiss the ways in which colonial legacy and current policy contributes to poverty and marginalisation (2012: 4; 12; compare with Schneider and Ingram 1997).

Western researchers' views on how to produce high-quality scientific evidence lead them to 'see indigenous peoples, their values and practices as political hindrances that get in the way of good research' (2012: xi; 66–71). Similarly, the combination of a state's formal laws and unwritten rules and assumptions can serve to dismiss indigenous community knowledge as not meeting their evidential standards, and indigenous researchers as less technically proficient (2012: 44–9; 12).

Decolonising Policy-Relevant Research

In that context, Smith (2012: xiii; 111–25) outlines a new agenda built on the recognition that research is connected explicitly to political and policy aims, not objective science (2012: xiii). It connects research directly to indigenous community 'self-determination', 'survival', 'recovery', and 'development', aided by processes such as social movement mobilisation and decolonisation (2012: 121). This agenda informs the meaning of ethical conduct, signalling that research: serves explicit emancipatory goals, requires distinctive methods and practices to produce knowledge, and requires a code of respectful conduct (2012: 124; 179–81). Although not focused directly on policy analysis, a decolonising project informs directly the 'steps' to policy analysis described above.

First, it affects problem definition. It establishes the value of co-producing problem definition with indigenous peoples. Mintrom (2012) describes the moral and practical value of engaging with stakeholders to help frame policy problems and design solutions (to transform and improve the world). However, Smith (2012: 228–32; 13) describes such a profound gulf, in the framing of problems, that will not be bridged simply via consultation or half-hearted 'co-production' exercises.

For example, if a government policy analyst relates poor health to individual and cultural factors in indigenous communities, and people in those communities relate it to colonisation, land confiscation, minimal self-determination, and an excessive focus on individuals, what could we realistically expect from set-piece government-led stakeholder analyses built on research that has already set the policy agenda? Rather, Smith (2012: 15–16) describes the need for continuous respect for a community's 'cultural protocols, values and behaviours' as part of 'an ethical and respectful approach'. Indeed, the latter could have mutual benefits which underpin the long-term development of trust: a community may feel less marginalised by the analysis-to-policy process, and future analysts may be viewed with less suspicion. Even so, a more respectful policy process is not the same as accepting that some communities may benefit more from writing about their own experiences than contributing to someone else's story. Writing about the past, present, and future is an exercise of power to provide a dominant perspective with which to represent people and problems (2012: 29–41; 52–9).

Second, it affects how analysts generate and compare solutions. Imagine a cost-benefit analysis designed to identify the most efficient outcomes by translating all of the predicted impacts on people into a single unit of analysis (such as a dollar amount, or quality-adjusted-life-years). Cost-benefit assumptions include that we can: (a) assign the same value to a notionally similar experience and (b) produce winners from policy and compensate losers. Yet, this calculation hinges on the power to decide how we should understand such experiences and place relative values on outcomes, and to take a calculation of their value to one population and generalise it to others. Smith's analysis suggests that such processes will not produce outcomes that we can describe honestly as societal improvements. Rather, they feed into a choice to produce winners from policy and fail to compensate losers in an adequate or appropriate manner.

The Limits to Truly Co-produced Policy Analysis (in the Absence of Radical Change)

Smith's (2012) analysis, coupled with wider insights from core texts on power, should also prompt us to be sceptical about the extent to which policy analysis can be improved with slight modifications and without radical political and social change. If so, any rhetoric on new forms of policy analysis may perform the opposite role, to *look* progressive as a substitute for action.

Can We Describe Policy Analysis Processes as 'Co-production' if There Is Such an Imbalance of Power and Incongruence of Ideas Between Participants?

One issue with very quick client-oriented policy analysis is that it encourages analysts to (a) work with an already-chosen definition of the policy problem and (b) use well-worn methods to collect information, including (c) engaging with ideas and people with whom they are already familiar.

Some forms of research and policy analysis may be more conducive to challenging existing frames and encouraging wider stakeholder engagement. Still, compare this mild shift from the status quo with a series of issues and possibilities identified by Lorde (2018):

- The 'European-American male tradition' only allows for narrowly defined ('rational') means of communication, which marginalise many groups (2018: 6–15).

Some people are so marginalised and dismissed that they struggle to communicate—about the ways in which they are oppressed, and how they might contribute to imagining a better world—in ways that would be valued (or even noticed) during stakeholder consultation (2018: 1–5).

- A forum can be designed *ostensibly* to foster communication and inclusivity, only to actually produce the opposite.

Poorly designed processes can signal to some participants that they are a token afterthought, whose views and experiences are of limited relevance, or too challenging to incorporate. If so, they prompt marginalised people to work hard simply to be heard. They learn that powerful people are only willing to listen if others do the work for them, because (a) they *are ignorant* of experiences other than their own and/or (b) they *profess ignorance strategically* to suck the energy from people whose views they fear and do not understand (2018: 16–21).

- The correct response to racism and colonisation is anger.

Therefore, do not prioritise (a) narrow rules of civility, or the sensibilities of the privileged, if (b) your aim is to encourage conversations with people who are trying to express the ways in which they deal with overwhelming and continuous hatred, violence, and oppression (2018: 22–35).

Are Such Forms of Policy Analysis a Deliberate Substitute for Changes to Political Practices?
Why might your potential allies in 'co-produced policy analysis' be suspicious of your motives, or sceptical about the likely outcomes of such an exchange? One theme throughout Smith's (2012) book is that people often co-opt key terms (such as 'decolonising') to perform the sense that they care about social change, to try to *look like* they are doing something important, while actually designing ineffective or bad faith processes to protect the status of themselves or their own institution or profession. Ahmed (2017: 103) describes comparable initiatives—such as to foster 'equality and diversity'—as a public relations exercise for organisations, rather than a sincere desire to do the work. Consequently, there is a gap 'between a symbolic commitment and a lived reality' (2017: 90). Indeed, the aim may be to project a sense of transformation to hinder that transformation (2017: 90). It comes with a tendency to use a 'safe' and non-confrontational language ('diversity') to project the sense that we can only push people so far, at the expense of terms such as 'racism' that would signal challenge, confrontation, and a commitment to high impact (2017: chapter 4).

Does the Production of a Common Agreement Simply Hide Inequalities of Power?
Imagine policy analysis at a global level, in which some countries and international organisations negotiate agreements, influenced in a limited way by critical social movements in pursuit of social justice. Santos (2014) identifies a series of obstacles including:

- Western (or Global North) ways of thinking dominate analysis, at the expense of insights from the Global South (2014: viii)
- 'Western-centric' ideas promote the sense that some concepts and collective aims—such as human dignity and human rights—can be understood universally, rather than through the lens of struggles that are specific to some regions (2014: 21; 38)
- A lack of imagination or willingness to imagine different futures and conceptions of social justice (2014: 24).

Consequently, policy actors may come together to discuss major policy change on ostensibly the same terms, only for some groups to—intentionally *and* unintentionally—dominate thought and action and reinforce the global inequalities they propose to reduce.

Such insights suggest that a stated commitment to co-produce research and policy *might* begin with good intentions. Even so, a commitment to sincere engagement does not guarantee an audience or prevent you from exacerbating the very problems you profess to solve.

Power Is Inherent in the Description of Good Knowledge

Previous sections show how the assertion of scientific objectivity and the superiority of scientific evidence create barriers between indigenous knowledge and policy. Yet, as Hindess (1977: 3–22) shows, all claims to knowledge are flawed because they involve inescapable circularity: we employ philosophy to identify the nature of the world (ontology) and how humans can generate valid knowledge of it (epistemology) to inform methodology, to state that scientific knowledge is only valid if it lives up to a prescribed method. Then, we argue that scientific knowledge validates the methodology and its underlying philosophy (1977: 3–22). If so, we are describing something that makes sense according to the rules and practices of its proponents, not an objective scientific method to help us accumulate knowledge. Further, the generation of different forms of knowledge, based on different rules and practices, raises the prospect that approaches to knowledge may be 'incommensurable', without a clear way to adjudicate between them. If different approaches do not share 'a common set of perceptions' (or even a set of comparable questions) 'which would allow scientists to choose between one paradigm and the other … there will be disputes between them that cannot all be settled by an appeal to the facts' (Hindess 1988: 74). Therefore, 'there is no possibility of an extratheoretical court of appeal which can "validate" the claims of one position against those of another' (Hindess 1977: 226).

If so, one can simply *assert* the primacy of scientific evidence or reject such dogma, to reflect on the production, purpose, value, and limitations of our knowledge in different contexts. On that basis, we can have honest discussions about why we should exercise power in a political system to favour some forms of knowledge over others in policy analysis, reflecting on:

1. *Internal consistency*: is an approach coherent, and does it succeed on its own terms?

   - For example, do its users share a clear language, pursue consistent aims with systematic methods, find ways to compare and reinforce the value of each other's findings, while contributing to a thriving research agenda (Heikkila and Cairney 2018)?
   - Or, do they express their aims in other ways, such as to connect research to emancipation, or value respect for a community over the scientific study of that community?

2. *Collaborative consistency*: how can we compare different forms of knowledge when they do not follow each other's rules or standards?

   - What if one approach is more rigorous and the other more coherent?
   - What if one produces more data, but another produces more understanding and ownership?

3. *Synthesising knowledge*: Spiegelhalter (2018) provides a convincing description of the benefits of systematic review and 'meta-analysis' within a single, clearly defined, scientific approach containing high agreement on methods and standards for comparison. However, this approach is not applicable directly to the review of multiple forms of knowledge. Some systematic reviewers make the mistake of applying the methodological standards of their own field to all others. Policy analysts are more likely to apply different criteria—is it available, understandable, 'usable', and policy relevant—but with similar problems of inclusion and exclusion.

In each case, the choice of criteria for comparing forms of knowledge involves political choice, without the ability—described in relation to cost-benefit analysis—to translate all relevant factors into a single unit. Analysts choose to include/exclude certain forms of knowledge according to professional norms or policymaking imperatives, not a technical process to identify the most objective information.

Policy Analysis for Marginalised Groups

Doucet (2019: 1) draws on such insights to identify three guiding questions, to show how to improve the use of evidence and knowledge in policy analysis. First, *for what purposes do policymakers find evidence useful?* Examples include to: inform a definition of problems and solutions, foster practitioner-learning, support an existing political position, or impose programmes backed by evidence. Second, *who decides what to use, and what is useful?* Actors determining usefulness could be the researchers providing evidence, the policymakers using it, the stakeholders involved in co-production, or the people affected by research and policy. Third, *how do critical theories inform these questions?* They remind us that so-called rational policy processes have incorporated research evidence to help: 'maintain power hierarchies and accept social inequity as a given. Indeed, research has been historically and contemporaneously (mis)used to justify a range of social harms' (2019: 2). Further, they help us redefine usefulness in relation to: 'how well research evidence communicates the lived experiences of marginalized groups' (2019: 3).

In that context, Doucet (2019) recommends a collection of responses, to:

1. *Recognise the ways in which research, policy analysis, and policy combine to reproduce the subordination of social groups.* General mechanisms include the reproduction of the assumptions, norms, and rules that produce a disproportionate impact on social groups (compare with Schneider and Ingram 2005). Specific mechanisms include judging marginalised groups harshly according to 'Western, educated, industrialized, rich and democratic' norms ('WEIRD').
2. *Reject the idea that scientific research can be seen as objective or neutral,* and that researchers are beyond reproach for their role in subordination and marginalisation.
3. *Give proper recognition to 'experiential knowledge' and 'transdisciplinary approaches' to knowledge production,* rather than privileging scientific knowledge.

4. *Commit to social justice*, to help 'eliminate oppressions and to emancipate and empower marginalized groups', such as by disrupting 'the policies and practices that disproportionately harm marginalized groups' (2019: 5–7).
5. *Develop strategies to 'centre race'*, 'democratise' research production, and 'leverage' transdisciplinary methods (including poetry, oral history and narrative, art, and discourse analysis) (2019: 10–22).

Michener (2019) provides a framework to understand the policymaking context in which such approaches interact, to identify the rules, norms, and practices that reinforce subordination. Michener's (2019: 424) 'racialized feedback framework (RFF)' helps explain the 'unrelenting force with which racism and White supremacy have pervaded social, economic, and political institutions in the United States'. Key mechanisms include (2019: 424–6):

1. 'Channelling resources', in which the rules, to distribute government resources, benefit some social groups and punish others. Examples include privileging White populations in social security schemes and the design/provision of education and punishing Black populations disproportionately in prisons (2019: 428–32). These rules also influence the motivation of social groups to engage in politics to influence policy (some citizens are emboldened, others alienated).
2. 'Generating interests', in which 'racial stratification' is a key factor in the power of interest groups (and balance of power in them).
3. 'Shaping interpretive schema', in which race is a lens through which actors understand, interpret, and seek to solve policy problems.
4. The ways in which centralisation (making policy at the federal level) or decentralisation influence policy design. For example, the 'historical record' suggests that decentralisation is more likely to 'be a force of inequality than an incubator of power for people of color' (2019: 433).

Revisiting the Pragmatic Client-Oriented Policy Analyst

This type of analysis provides a profound challenge to common policy analysis advice. Most policy analysis textbooks advocate pragmatism. Classic texts focus on client-oriented steps, to produce just enough policy-relevant information to help define problems and identify solutions. Make sure that your client-oriented advice builds on your client's timetable and definition of the problem. Manage your expectations about your ability to change policy (and influence policymaking). In *that old context*, pragmatism relates to the idea that policy analysis consists of 'art and craft', in which analysts assess what is politically feasible if taking a low-risk client-oriented approach.

In *this new context*, pragmatism is a euphemism for conservatism, as an excuse to reject ambitious and necessary plans for policy change. For example, the identification of colonisation and systematic racism, from the production of knowledge to its use in policy analysis to produce racist policy and institutions, warns us about the role of policy analysis in maintaining the status quo. This focus on the wider political context prompts us to reflect further on the relationship between power and policy-relevant information, when we decide whose knowledge counts. People exercise power to tell stories that benefit some and punish others, and they draw on limited sources of knowledge to make their case.

Such descriptions of policy analysis also reinforce studies of power, which suggest that the most profound and worrying kinds of power are the hardest to observe (Cairney 2020: 44–54). First, actors use their resources to reinforce social attitudes and policymakers' beliefs, to establish which issues are policy problems worthy of attention and which populations deserve government support or punishment. Second, studies of power relate these processes to the manipulation of ideas or shared beliefs, to identify the public interest or encourage social norms which are enforced by the state, social groups, and individuals who govern their own behaviour with reference to what they feel is expected of them. Such beliefs, norms, and rules are profoundly important because they often remain unspoken and taken for granted in everyday practices. If so, we may not need to identify manipulative policy analysts to find unequal power relationships: strong and enduring social practices help some people win at the expense of others. Third, they identify the act of dismissing an individual, social group, or population by undermining the value of their knowledge or claim to knowledge.

In that context, this chapter identifies the ways in which policy analysis can challenge such strategies while doing their work. Acknowledge inequalities in relation to marginalised populations, and pay more attention to inequalities in research and practice (Doucet 2019; Michener 2019). Do not treat policy analysis simply as a pragmatic client-oriented activity, because this perspective misses this bigger picture and contributes to the practices that help maintain inequalities. In other words, it goes against a wider policy analysis professional commitment to 'speak truth to power' to foster 'human dignity'.

References

Ahmed, S. (2017). *Living a Feminist Life*. Durham: Duke University Press.

Bacchi, C. (2009). *Analysing Policy: What's the problem represented to be?* Frenchs Forest, NSW: Pearson.

Cairney, P. (2019). The UK Government's Imaginative Use of Evidence to Make Policy. *British Politics, 14*(1), 1–22.

Cairney, P. (2020). *Understanding Public Policy* (2nd ed.). London: Red Globe.

Cairney, P., & Kwiatkowski, R. (2017). How to Communicate Effectively with Policymakers: Combine Insights from Psychology and Policy Studies. *Palgrave Communications, 3*, 37. Retrieved from https://www.nature.com/articles/s41599-017-0046-8.

Cairney, P., Oliver, K., & Wellstead, A. (2016). To Bridge the Divide between Evidence and Policy: Reduce Ambiguity as Much as Uncertainty. *Public Administration Review, 76*(3), 399–402.

Doucet, F. (2019). *Centering the Margins: (Re)defining Useful Research Evidence Through Critical Perspectives*. New York: William T. Grant Foundation.

Heikkila, T., & Cairney, P. (2018). Comparison of Theories of the Policy Process. In C. Weible & P. Sabatier (Eds.), *Theories of the Policy Process* (4th ed.). Chicago: Westview Press.

Hindess, B. (1977). *Philosophy and Methodology in the Social Sciences*. Hemel Hempstead: Harvester.

Hindess, B. (1988). *Choice, Rationality and Social Theory*. London: Unwin Hyman.

Hogwood, B. (1987). *From Crisis to Complacency*. Oxford: Oxford University Press.

Jones, M., Shanahan, E., & McBeth, M. (Eds.). (2014). *The Science of Stories: Applications of the Narrative Policy Framework in Public Policy Analysis*. New York: Palgrave.

Lorde, A. (2018). *The Master's Tools Will Never Dismantle the Master's House*. London: Penguin.

Lubell, M. (2013). Governing Institutional Complexity: The Ecology of Games Framework. *Policy Studies Journal, 41*(3), 537–559.

McConnell, A. (2010). *Understanding Policy Success: Rethinking Public Policy.* London: Red Globe Press.
Michener, J. (2019). Policy Feedback in a Racialized Polity. *Policy Studies Journal, 47*(2), 423–450.
Ostrom, E. (1990). *Governing the Commons: The Evolution of Institutions for Collective Action.* Cambridge: Cambridge University Press.
Ostrom, E. (2011). Background on the Institutional Analysis and Development Framework. *Policy Studies Journal, 39*(1), 7–27.
Riker, W. (1986). *The Art of Political Manipulation.* New Haven: Yale University Press.
Santos, B. (2014). *Epistemologies of the South: Justice Against Epistemicide.* New York: Routledge.
Schneider, A., & Ingram, H. (1997). *Policy Design for Democracy.* Kansas: University of Kansas Press.
Schneider, A., & Ingram, H. (Eds.). (2005). *Deserving and Entitled: Social Construction and Public Policy.* Albany: State University of New York Press.
Smith, L. T. (2012). *Decolonizing Methodologies* (2nd ed.). London: Zed Books.
Spiegelhalter, D. (2018). *The Art of Statistics: Learning from Data.* London: Pelican.
Stone, D. (2012). *Policy Paradox: The Art of Political Decision Making* (3rd ed.). London: Norton.
Streeck, W., & Thelen, K. (Eds.). (2005). *Beyond Continuity: Institutional Change in Advanced Political Economies.* Oxford: Oxford University Press.
Thibodeau, P., & Boroditsky, L. (2011). Metaphors We Think With: The Role of Metaphor in Reasoning. *Plos One.* https://doi.org/10.1371/journal.pone.0016782.

CHAPTER 6

How Have *How to Do* Policy Analysis Texts Incorporated These Insights So Far?

Abstract Modern policy analysis texts incorporate many developments in the study of policy processes. They describe the gap between what policy analysts need policymakers to do and what policymakers can actually do. Still, they remain committed to simple and pragmatic guides, informed by insights on knowledge production and policy process research, but without imagining new forms of policy analysis.

Keywords Policy analysis • Art and craft of policy analysis • Communication • Policy analysis ethics

INTRODUCTION

Policy analysis texts now reflect many of these developments *somewhat*, in new editions of classics, or new approaches. For example, Dunn's (2017) general advice to be pragmatic is based on policy process insights. He contrasts the 'art and craft' (Wildavsky 1980) of policy analysis with the idea of 'evidence-based policymaking'. The naïve attachment to 'facts speak for themselves' or 'knowledge for its own sake' undermines a researcher's ability to adapt well to the evidence-demands of policymakers (Dunn 2017: 68; 4). In practice, analysis is influenced by: the cognitive shortcuts that analysts use to gather information; the role they perform in an organisation; the time constraints and incentive structures in

© The Author(s), under exclusive license to Springer Nature Switzerland AG 2021
P. Cairney, *The Politics of Policy Analysis*,
https://doi.org/10.1007/978-3-030-66122-9_6

organisations and political systems; the expectations and standards of their profession; and the need to work with teams consisting of many professions/disciplines (2017: 15–6). The cost, in terms of time and resources, of conducting multiple research and analytical methods is high, and highly constrained in political environments (2017: 17–8). Therefore, note the value of 'erotetic rationality' in which people deal with their lack of knowledge of a complex world by giving up on the idea of certainty (accepting their 'ignorance'), in favour of a continuous process of 'questioning and answering' (2017: 47–52).

Similarly, Weimer and Vining (2017) highlight a gap between (a) our ability to model and predict economic and social behaviour and (b) what actually happens when governments intervene. They describe the need to supplement a 'solid grounding' in economics and statistics with political awareness, and the 'development of a professional mind-set' rather than perfecting 'technical skills' (2017: 30; 34–40). This approach requires some knowledge of policy theories, and they discuss: (a) theory-inspired *strategies* including 'co-optation', 'compromise', 'rhetoric', and 'heresthetics', (b) the role of *narrative* in 'writing implementation scenarios', and (c) the need to address the *complexity* of mixing many policy interventions (2017: 259–323). Note how flexible this advice must be, to reflect factors such as:

- the (unpredictable) effect that different clients and contexts have on your task
- the pressure on your limited time and resources
- the ambiguity of broad goals such as equity and human dignity
- a tendency of your clients to (a) not know, or (b) choose not to reveal their goals before you complete your analysis of possible policy solutions (2017: 347–9)
- the need to balance many factors—(a) answering your client's question with confidence, (b) describing uncertainty, and (c) recognising the benefit of humility—to establish your reputation as a provider of credible and reliable analysis (2017: 341; 363; 373; 453).

Flexible Communication

Further, Smith's (2015) advice on communication rests upon knowledge of policy processes guides. First, Smith (2015) advises that there is no linear and orderly policy cycle in which to present written analysis. The policymaking environment is more complex and less predictable than this model suggests. Consequently, there is no blueprint or uniform template for writing policy analysis. The mix of policy problems is too diverse to manage with one approach, and 'context' may be more important than the 'content' of your proposal. Communication comes in many forms to reflect many possible venues.

Second, policy communication is not a rational/technical process. It is a political exercise, built on the use of values to frame and try to solve problems. Analysis takes place in often highly divisive debates. People communicate using stories, and they use framing and persuasion techniques. They need to tailor their arguments to specific audiences, rather than hoping that one document could appeal to everyone. Everyone may have the ability to frame issues, but only some policymakers 'have authority to decide' to pay attention to and interpret problems.

Ethical and Normative Responses

Mintrom (2012: 5–7) focuses more on policy analyst conduct and professionalism. He describes Radin's narrative regarding the changing nature of policy analysis, in which there is now a much larger profession, spread across—and outside of—government, engaging explicitly in the politics of policy analysis and advice. If so, any advice on how to do policy analysis has to be flexible, to incorporate the greater diversity of actors and the sense that complex policymaking systems require flexible skills and practices rather than standardised techniques and outputs.

In that context, Mintrom (2012: 95–108) emphasises the enduring role for *ethical* policy analysis, which can relate to *'universal' principles* such as fairness, compassion, and respect, *specific principles* to project the analyst's integrity, competence, responsibility, respectfulness, and concern for others, and new professional and analytical strategies. New *professional practices* include to:

- engage with many stakeholders in problem definition, to reflect a diversity of knowledge and views
- present a range of feasible solutions, making clear their distributional effects on target populations, opportunity costs (what policies/outcomes would *not* be funded if this were), and impact on those who implement policy

- be honest about (a) the method of calculation and (b) uncertainty, when projecting outcomes
- clarify the trade-offs between alternatives (don't stack-up the evidence for one), and maximise effective information sharing, rather than exploiting the limited attention of your audience.

New analytical strategies (2012: 114–15; 246–84) include the analysis of factors such as gender and race, to: measure the extent to which social groups are already 'systematically disadvantaged'; identify the causes (such as racism and sexism) of, and potential solutions to, these outcomes; make sure that new policies reduce or do not perpetuate disadvantages; discourage politicians from trying to gain electorally from scapegoating target populations; and encourage transformative policy change even when there are major obstacles.

Weimer and Vining emphasise the client orientation, which limits your time, freedom, and perhaps inclination to challenge strongly the problem definitions that punish powerless populations. Still, this normative role is part of an ethical duty to:

- balance a 'responsibility to client' with 'analytical integrity' and 'adherence to one's personal conception of the good society', and challenge the client if they undermine professional values (2017: 43–50),
- reflect on the extent to which a policy analyst should seek to be an 'Objective Technician', 'Client's Advocate', or 'Issue Advocate' (2017: 44; see also Chap. 9),
- recognise the highly political nature of seemingly technical processes such as cost-benefit analysis (2017: 403–6), and
- encourage politicians to put 'aside their narrow personal and political interests for the greater good' (2017: 454).

Still, Policy Analysis Texts Remain Attached to Five-Step Guides

Meltzer and Schwartz (2019: 1–3) provide the most recent and spirited defence of five-step policy analysis, arguing that their critics provide no useful alternative to help guide new policy analysts. These guides are essential:

to be persuasive, and credible, analysts must situate the problem, defend their evaluative criteria, and be able to demonstrate that their policy recommendation is superior, on balance, to other alternative options in addressing the problem, as defined by the analyst. At a minimum, the analyst needs to present a clear and defensible ranking of options to guide the decisions of the policy makers. (Meltzer and Schwartz 2019: 4)

In other words, the problem is a too-rigid 'rationalistic approach' to five-step policy analysis, which can be solved by a 'flexible' and 'iterative' approach. Meltzer and Schwartz (2019: 27–8) explore ways to *improve* rather than replace a five-step model, using insights from approaches such as 'design thinking'. *This commitment to maintaining simple and pragmatic guides, informed by insights on knowledge production and policy process research, helps set the stage for part two of this book.*

References

Dunn, W. (2017). *Public Policy Analysis* (6th ed.). Routledge.
Meltzer, R., & Schwartz, A. (2019). *Policy Analysis as Problem Solving*. London: Routledge.
Mintrom, M. (2012). *Contemporary Policy Analysis*. Oxford: Oxford University Press.
Smith, C. (2015). *Writing Public Policy*. Oxford University Press.
Weimer, D., & Vining, A. (2017). *Policy Analysis: Concepts and Practice* (6th ed.). London: Routledge.
Wildavsky, A. (1980). *The Art and Craft of Policy Analysis*. London: Macmillan.

PART II

Challenging Themes in Policy Analysis

Part II presents a collection of themes on the role of policy analysis in complex policymaking environments, in which the nature of evidence and nature of policy problems is highly contested, and policy analysis can reinforce the inequalities that analysts may seek to reduce. Policy analysts face constant dilemmas because there will always necessarily be trade-offs between aims, such as to recognise policy and policymaking complexity but find ways to simplify analysis, to recognise profound socioeconomic inequalities but not describe policy problems as too large to solve, and to seek major policy change but be pragmatic in relation to your audience. What can they do, and what should they do, when they face such dilemmas?

CHAPTER 7

Comparing What You Need as a Policy Analyst with Policymaking Reality

Abstract This chapter challenges a tendency to equate what policymakers and analysts *need*, to do their job effectively, and what they can actually *expect to happen*. It revisits Lasswell's distinction between policy process research, as the analysis *of* policy, and policy analysis as the analysis *for* policy. Both provide different answers to key questions such as: does policymaking actually proceed through a series of steps or stages?

Keywords Policy analysis • Analysis of policy • Analysis for policy • Lasswell • Policy cycle and stages

INTRODUCTION

Our first key theme regards a tendency to equate what policymakers and analysts need, to do their job effectively, and what they can actually expect to happen. To demonstrate, it is worth revisiting Lasswell's distinction between policy process research, as the analysis *of* policy, and policy analysis as the analysis *for* policy. Although Lasswell highlighted the value of combining their insights, in doing so we should be careful not to confuse the two. The lines between each approach may be blurry, and each element makes less sense without the other, but the distinction is crucial to help us overcome the major confusion associated with this question:

Does Policymaking Actually Proceed Through a Series of Stages?

The short answer is no, but you may be forgiven for thinking that it does. The longer answer is that almost all of the field of policy studies (a) treat the stage-based model—the policy cycle—as akin to an ideal-type and (b) compare it with descriptions of real-world policymaking. In a nutshell, most policy theorists reject the policy image because it oversimplifies a complex policymaking system (Fig. 4.1, p. 54). Indeed, I argue that it does more harm than good, for two main reasons (Cairney 2020):

1. Descriptively, it is inaccurate, unless you imagine thousands of policy cycles interacting with each other to produce less orderly behaviour and less predictable outputs (Fig. 4.1).
2. Prescriptively, it gives you misleading advice about the nature of your policymaking task.

If the Policy Cycle Does Not Exist, Why Does the Image Persist?

Common reasons include that the stage-based approach provides one way to *introduce* policy studies (Wu et al. 2017), relate it to policy analysis (Althaus et al. 2013; Hogwood and Gunn 1984), use it as a learning aid or initial heuristic for practitioners (Threlfall and Althaus 2020), and project policymaking order to the public (Cairney 2015). The simple model of a cycle with stages might endure because it can help policymakers and practitioners understand their task in the simplest way, then describe what to do. The world is complex, but policymakers have to simplify it to take action *and* to explain their account to the legislatures and public to which they are accountable (Cairney 2015: 26). Or, at least, they must tell a story of what they'd like to do: identify their aims, identify policies to achieve those aims, select a policy measure, ensure that the selection is legitimised by the population or its legislature, identify the necessary resources, implement, then evaluate the policy. All the while, you can hold them to account because they are in control. Indeed, imagine the alternative: policymakers tell the public that the policy process is too complicated to understand and explain what they are doing.

Yet, as far as I can tell, policymakers don't tell this cycle story as consistently as they used to. Further, key organisations such as the European Commission tell a much different story about the need to accept and respond to policymaking complexity (Topp et al. 2018). In that context, for present purposes, I suggest two further explanations:

1. *It arose from a misunderstanding in policy studies*

Weible and Cairney (2019) argue the stages approach represents a good idea gone wrong. If you trace it back to its origins, you will find Lasswell's (1956) description of decision functions: intelligence, recommendation, prescription, invocation, application, appraisal, and termination. These functions correspond reasonably well to a policy cycle's stages: agenda setting, formulation, legitimation, implementation, evaluation, and maintenance, succession, or termination. However, Weible and Cairney (2019) argue that the stages morphed into a cycle as Lasswell's ideas became popular in texts by Lasswell-inspired scholars. For example, Jones (1970) established the term 'policy cycle', Brewer (1974: 240) replaced the decision functions with 'six basic phases through which a policy or program passes over time', and other books organised chapters according to stages in a cycle (Anderson 1975; May and Wildavsky 1978; Brewer and deLeon 1983).

2. *It describes functional requirements of policy analysis*

However, Lasswell was imagining *functional requirements*, while the cycle seems to describe *actual stages* (Weible and Cairney 2019; Dunn 2017: 42–3). In other words, if you take Lasswell's list of what policy analysts and many policymakers need to do, multiply it by the number of actors (spread across many organisations or venues) trying to do it, then you get the complex (or 'multi-centric') policy processes described by modern theories (see Cairney et al. 2019). If, instead, you strip all that activity down into a single cycle, you get the wrong idea.

In that context, studies of policy analysis in action suggest that (a) an individual analyst's *need for simple steps*, to turn policymaking complexity into useful heuristics and pragmatic strategies, should not be confused with *what actually happens* when many policy analysts, influencers, and policymakers interact in policy processes. Just to hammer home the point, note a major difference between:

1. *Functional requirements.* What you need from policymaking systems, to (a) manage your task (the five-step policy analysis) and (b) understand and engage in policy processes (the simple policy cycle).
2. *Actual processes and outcomes.* What policy concepts and theories tell us about bounded rationality (which limit the comprehensiveness of your analysis) and policymaking complexity (which undermines your understanding and engagement in policy processes).

Policy analysis takes place in a policymaking environment over which no one has full knowledge or control. There is no all-powerful 'centre' able to control policy outcomes via a series of steps in a policy cycle. Rather, as Dunn (2017: 44–5) suggests, if we must maintain a focus on notional 'stages', think of them as interacting continuously and often out of order. Attention to a policy problem fluctuates, actors propose and adopt solutions continuously, actors are making policy (and feeding back on its success) as they implement, evaluation of policy success is not a single-shot document, and previous policies set the agenda for new policy. In that context, it is no surprise that the impact of a single policy analysis is usually minimal (2017: 57).

What Do You Need to Define a Policy Problem, and What Types of Solutions Are Available?

This distinction between (a) the functional requirements of policy analysis and (b) the real-world constraints described in policy process research helps us understand the role of problem definition and solution development in a highly political and complex policy process. It prompts us to ask who exactly our audience is when we define problems, and what we can realistically expect them to do with our solutions.

Defining Problems: Clients and Environments

The classic five-step policy analysis texts focus on how to define policy problems *well*, but they vary somewhat in their definition of doing it well. Bardach (2012) recommends using rhetoric and eye-catching data to generate attention. Weimer and Vining (2017) and Mintrom (2012) recommend beginning with your client's 'diagnosis', placing it in a wider perspective to help analyse it critically, and asking yourself how else you might define it. Meltzer and Schwartz (2019) and Dunn (2017) identify additional ways to contextualise your client's definition, such as by generating a timeline to help 'map' causation or using 'problem-structuring methods' to compare definitions and avoid making too many assumptions on a problem's cause. Thissen (2013) compares 'rational' and 'argumentative' approaches, treating problem definition as something to be measured scientifically or established rhetorically.

As such, these texts identify analytical techniques but recognise that problem definition is not simply a technical process to be broken down into a series of unproblematic steps. Rather, critical studies emphasise the role of power and politics to determine whose knowledge is relevant (Smith 2012) and whose problem definition counts (Bacchi 2009; Stone 2012). Problem definition is a political act, to try to establish whose interests matter, how they see the world, and what counts as good or bad evidence.

Policy process research also describes problem definition and agenda setting in relation to framing, narrative, social construction, and power (Baumgartner and Jones 2009; Cairney 2020: 154–9; Jones et al. 2014; Schneider and Ingram 1997). Actors exercise power to try to generate attention to their policy problem at the expense of others, and for their preferred frame at the expense of other interpretations. Success helps them translate their beliefs into policy, by fostering or undermining policy change. It requires them to persuade powerful audiences, by drawing on insights from psychology to understand how policymakers might combine cognition and emotion to understand problems (Cairney and Kwiatkowski 2017). In other words, focus on persuasion to reduce ambiguity (when there are many ways to interpret problems) rather than simply the provision of information to reduce uncertainty (when there is low knowledge) (Cairney 2019; Zahariadis 2007: 66).

What these accounts have in common is that they raise normative questions about how analysts should engage with clients. For example, should they accept or push boundaries? Should they accept the ways in which their clients understand problems, and try to provide new information on that basis, or challenge this framing as part of a challenge to the status quo (which perpetuates an unequal balance of power and resources)?

However, if we stop there, *we generate a misleading impression regarding the extent to which this choice is in the gift of the analyst* (or indeed the policymaker). In this context, the key insight from policy studies is that policy is not made by a small group of actors aided by an elite cadre of analysts. Rather, policy analysis has become a much wider competition between analysts as advocates, in an environment over which no one has full understanding or control. In other words, if we shift our analysis from analysts/clients towards environments and systems, we generate a very different image of the constraints and opportunities associated with each role (see Chap. 12, "How Far Would You Go to Secure Impact from Your Analysis?").

Producing Solutions as Part of a Policy Mix
The classic five-step policy analysis emphasises technical and political aspects to solution production:

- *Technical feasibility.* Will a solution work as intended, given the alleged severity and cause of the problem?
- *Political feasibility.* Will it receive sufficient support from my client, given the ways in which key policy actors weigh up the costs and benefits of action?

Put simply, (a) a technocratic choice about the 'optimality' of a solution is useless without considering who will support its adoption, and (b) some types of solution will always be a hard sell, no matter their alleged effectiveness. Bardach (2012) recommends identifying solutions that your audience might consider, perhaps providing a range of options on a notional spectrum of acceptability. Smith (2015) highlights the value of 'precedent', or relating potential solutions to previous strategies. Weimer and Vining (2017) identify the importance of 'a professional mind-set' that may be more important than perfecting 'technical skills'. Mintrom (2012) notes that some solutions are easier to sell than others. Meltzer and Schwartz (2019) describe the benefits of making a preliminary recommendation to inform an iterative process, drawing feedback from clients and stakeholder groups. Dunn (2017) warns against too narrow forms of 'evidence-based' analysis which undermine a researcher's ability to adapt well to the evidence-demands of policymakers. In each case, the solution depends on how analysts frame the problem. For example, if you define tobacco and smoking in relation to: (a) its economic benefits, a solution relates to how to maximise export and taxation revenues; while (b) framing it as the cause of a global public health epidemic only prompts solutions that reduce in smoking in the population (Cairney 2016).

Policy studies go further. First, they ask: *what types of policy tools or instruments are actually used?* The answer can vary dramatically. For example, Cairney and St Denny (2020: 17–18) find that the same basic commitment—to so-called 'prevention policy'—can involve two profoundly different uses of policy instruments. At one end of the spectrum, we find the potential for 'maximal' commitment, when policymakers combine new regulations with redistributional tax and spending and a new policy-making organisation to oversee delivery. At the other, we find 'minimal' commitment based primarily on a government coordinating the sharing of information to encourage other actors to change their approach. In such cases, the lesson for analysts is that it is relatively easy to identify immediate political feasibility for a vague commitment to a new strategy, but significant policy change requires more than successful single-shot analyses (2020: 238).

Second, *how does the adoption of a new solution contribute to the size, substance, speed, and direction of policy change?* See Giordono and Cairney (2019) for a summary of common measures. What we call 'policy' is actually a collection of policy instruments. Governments already combine a large number of instruments to make policy, including legislation, expenditure, economic incentives and penalties, education, and various forms of service delivery. Those instruments combine to represent a complex policy mix whose overall effects are not simple to predict.

In some stories of policy change, each additional policy instrument is part of a comprehensive mix of instruments tied closely to a clear strategy (see Cairney et al. 2012 on stories of tobacco policy change). As such, they fulfil Lindblom's (1964, 1979) enduring and pervasive story about the benefits of policy analysis which advocates radical policy change via a series of non-radical (incremental) steps.

However, policy change is not so predictable or plannable. Most policy change is minor, but some is major, and the cause of major policy change is not simply in the gift of policymakers. Rather, the overall effect of a succession of individual policy changes is 'non-linear', difficult to predict, and subject to emergent outcomes, rather than cumulative (Spyridaki and Flamos 2014; Munro and Cairney 2020). This point is crucial to policy analysis: does the proposal of a new policy instrument merely add a new instrument to the pile, or necessitate a rethink of all instruments, to anticipate the disproportionate effect of a new policy instrument on the rest? It identifies essential context, particularly if you are asked to provide, say, a simple logic model or 'theory of change' to describe the likely impact of your new solution. The overall effect of policy is not so susceptible to prediction when governments add new policy solutions to an existing, complex, mix of solutions rather than working from a blank canvas.

Overall, the take-home message from this chapter is that policy analysis is incomplete without analysis of the policy process. For example, think of the policy process as a complex system that determines the impact of your solution. It can ensure that your intervention has a disproportionate impact on policy outcomes, from zero to profound. Policy analysts have limited control over the definition of a problem, and policymakers do not control the outcomes of their solutions. If so, this message could have a major impact on the role of policy analysis. In the next chapter, it prompts us to think about its normative role: if 'optimal' and evidence-based analysis is not possible, should analysts focus instead on public deliberation and stakeholder ownership ('the journey is more important than the destination')? In subsequent chapters, it prompts us to question the role of analysis more widely, to see how 'entrepreneurial' you can be, what exactly 'systems thinking' means in policy analysis, and ask how far you would go to secure policy attention and outcomes.

References

Althaus, C., Bridgman, P., & Davis, G. (2013). *The Australian Policy Handbook* (5th ed.). Sydney: Allen & Unwin.

Anderson, J. (1975). *Public Policy Making*. London: Thomas Nelson & Sons.

Bacchi, C. (2009). *Analysing Policy: What's the Problem Represented to Be?* NSW: Pearson.

Bardach, E. (2012). *A Practical Guide for Policy Analysis* (4th ed.). CQ Press.

Baumgartner, F., & Jones, B. (2009). *Agendas and Instability in American Politics* (2nd ed.). Chicago: University of Chicago Press.

Brewer, G. (1974). The Policy Sciences Emerge: To Nurture and Structure a Discipline. *Policy Sciences, 5*(3), 239–244.

Brewer, G., & deLeon, P. (1983). *The Foundations of Policy Analysis*. Chicago: Dorsey Press.

Cairney, P. (2015). How Can Policy Theory Have an Impact on Policy Making? *Teaching Public Administration, 33*(1), 22–39.

Cairney, P. (2016). *The Politics of Evidence-based Policymaking*. London: Palgrave Pivot.

Cairney, P. (2019). Fostering Evidence-Informed Policy Making: Uncertainty Versus Ambiguity. Quebec: National Collaborating Centre for Healthy Public Policy (NCCHPP). Retrieved from http://www.ncchpp.ca/165/Publications.ccnpps?id_article=1930.

Cairney, P. (2020). Taking Lessons from Policy Theory into Practice. In T. Mercer, B. Head, & J. Wanna (Eds.), *Learning Policy, Doing Policy: How Do Theories about Policymaking Influence Practice?* Canberra: ANU Press.

Cairney, P., Heikkila, T., & Wood, M. (2019). *Making Policy in a Complex World*. Cambridge: Cambridge University Press.
Cairney, P., & Kwiatkowski, R. (2017). How to Communicate Effectively with Policymakers: Combine Insights from Psychology and Policy Studies. *Palgrave Communications, 3*, 37. Retrieved from https://www.nature.com/articles/s41599-017-0046-8.
Cairney, P., & St Denny, E. (2020). *Why Isn't Government Policy More Preventive?* Oxford: Oxford University Press.
Cairney, P., Studlar, D., & Mamudu, H. (2012). *Global Tobacco Control*. Basingstoke: Palgrave Macmillan.
Dunn, W. (2017). *Public Policy Analysis* (6th ed.). Routledge.
Giordono, L., & Cairney, P. (2019). Policy Concepts in 1000 Words: How Do Policy Theories Describe Policy Change? *Paul Cairney: Politics & Public Policy*, August 11. Retrieved from https://paulcairney.wordpress.com/2019/08/11/policy-concepts-in-1000-words-how-do-policy-theories-describe-policy-change/.
Hogwood, B., & Gunn, L. (1984). *Policy Analysis for the Real World*. Oxford: Oxford University Press.
Jones, C. (1970). *An Introduction to the Study of Political Life*. Berkeley: Duxberry Press.
Jones, M., Shanahan, E., & McBeth, M. (Eds.). (2014). *The Science of Stories: Applications of the Narrative Policy Framework in Public Policy Analysis*. New York, NY: Palgrave Macmillan.
Lasswell, H. (1956). *The Decision Process: Seven Categories of Functional Analysis*. College Park, MD: University of Maryland Press.
Lindblom, C. (1964). Contexts for Change and Strategy: A Reply. *Public Administration Review, 24*(3), 157–158.
Lindblom, C. (1979). Still Muddling, Not Yet Through. *Public Administration Review, 39*(6), 517–525.
May, J., & Wildavsky, A. (1978). *The Policy Cycle*. Beverly Hills: Sage.
Meltzer, R., & Schwartz, A. (2019). *Policy Analysis as Problem Solving*. London: Routledge.
Mintrom, M. (2012). *Contemporary Policy Analysis*. Oxford: Oxford University Press.
Munro, F., & Cairney, P. (2020, March). A Systematic Review of Energy Systems: The Role of Policymaking in Sustainable Transitions. *Renewable & Sustainable Energy Reviews, 119*, 1–10.
Schneider, A., & Ingram, H. (1997). *Policy Design for Democracy*. Kansas: University of Kansas Press.
Smith, C. (2015). *Writing Public Policy*. Oxford University Press.
Smith, L. T. (2012). *Decolonizing Methodologies* (2nd ed.). London: Zed Books.

Spyridaki, N. A., & Flamos, A. (2014, December). A Paper Trail of Evaluation Approaches to Energy and Climate Policy Interactions. *Renewable and Sustainable Energy Reviews, 40*, 1090–1107.

Stone, D. (2012). *Policy Paradox: The Art of Political Decision Making* (3rd ed.). London: Norton.

Thissen, W. (2013). Diagnosing Policy Problem Situations. In W. Thissen & W. Walker (Eds.), *Public Policy Analysis: New Developments* (pp. 65–102). London: Springer.

Threlfall, D., & Althaus, C. (2020). A Quixotic Quest? Making Theory Speak to Practice. In T. Mercer, B. Head, & J. Wanna (Eds.), *Learning Policy, Doing Policy: How Do Theories About Policymaking Influence Practice?* Canberra: ANU Press.

Topp, L., Mair, D., Smillie, L., & Cairney, P. (2018). Knowledge Management for Policy Impact: The Case of the European Commission's Joint Research Centre. *Palgrave Communications, 4*, 87. https://doi.org/10.1057/s41599-018-0143-3.

Weible, C., & Cairney, P. (2019). A Diamond in the Rough: Digging up and Polishing Lasswell's Decision Functions. Paper prepared for the *Workshop on The Future of the Policy Sciences*, The Education University of Hong Kong, November 14–15.

Weimer, D., & Vining, A. (2017). *Policy Analysis: Concepts and Practice* (6th ed.). London: Routledge.

Wu, X., Howlett, M., Ramesh, M., & Fritzen, S. (2017). *The Public Policy Primer* (2nd ed.). London: Routledge.

Zahariadis, N. (2007). The Multiple Streams Framework. In P. Sabatier (Ed.), *Theories of the Policy Process*. Cambridge, MA: Westview Press.

CHAPTER 8

Who Should Be Involved in the Process of Policy Analysis?

Abstract This chapter compares two different approaches to the production of policy-relevant knowledge. 'Evidence-based policymaking' emphasises the role of a small number of experts synthesising evidence for policymakers. 'Co-production' emphasises the role of deliberation between a larger and more diverse group of people. These approaches are not mutually exclusive, but they present important trade-offs that no policy analyst should ignore.

Keywords Policy analysis • Evidence-based policymaking • Expertise • Synthesis • Co-production • Deliberation

INTRODUCTION

Policy analysis is a political act to decide who should be involved in the policy process. There are different visions of policy analysis, from a focus on 'evidence-based' policymaking built on research and expert knowledge, to a 'co-produced' exercise built on deliberation and multiple sources of knowledge. These choices are not *necessarily* mutually exclusive, but it is important to identify and address the potential tensions between them. Key issues include:

1. *How many people should be involved in policy analysis?* 'Evidence-based' analysis often suggests that we build policy with a small group of experts, while a 'co-produced' exercise builds on deliberation and wide inclusion (Cairney 2016). Further, as Dunlop and Radaelli (2018: 260) argue, a process of combining insights from many sources through deliberation (*reflective* learning) can also encourage wider cooperation on the rules and norms of policy engagement and delivery.
2. *Whose knowledge counts?* As discussed in Chap. 5, assigning value to knowledge is a political act that can reinforce inequalities when relying on a narrow range of scientific sources, or challenge inequalities when giving more respect to a wider range of academic and experiential sources.
3. *Who should control policy design?* For example, should policymaking be centralised, to roll out the allegedly 'best' instruments nationally, or decentralised, to allow the discretion to make different choices based on the same policy analysis?

Different answers to these questions have profoundly different implications for policy analysis. To demonstrate, let us begin with one simple story for each approach.

A Story of 'Evidence-Based Policymaking'

One story of 'evidence-based' policy analysis is that it should be based on the best available evidence of 'what works' (see Cairney 2016; Boaz et al. 2019). Often, the description of the 'best' evidence relates to the idea that there is a notional hierarchy of evidence according to the research methods used (Oliver and Pearce 2017). At the top would be the systematic review of randomised control trials, and at the bottom would be expertise, while practitioner knowledge and stakeholder feedback may not even feature (Althaus 2019: 4).

This kind of hierarchy has major implications for policy learning and transfer, such as when importing policy interventions from abroad or 'scaling up' domestic projects (see Rose 1993, 2005; Dolowitz and Marsh 1996, 2000). Put simply, the experimental method is designed to identify the causal effect of a very narrowly defined policy intervention. Its importation or scaling up would be akin to the description of medicine, in which the evidence identifies the causal effect of a specific active ingredient to be administered with the correct dosage. A very strong commitment to a uniform model precludes the consensus-seeking processes we might associate with co-production, in which many voices contribute to a policy design to suit a specific context (Cairney 2017; Cairney and Oliver 2017).

A Story of Co-production in Policymaking

One story of 'co-produced' policy analysis is that it should be based on respectful conversations between a wide range of policymakers and citizens. Often, descriptions emphasise the diversity of valuable policy-relevant information, with scientific evidence considered alongside experiential knowledge, community voices, and normative values. This rejection of a simple hierarchy of evidence also has major implications for policy learning and transfer. Put simply, a co-production method is designed to identify the positive effect—widespread 'ownership' of the problem and commitment to a commonly agreed solution—of a well-discussed intervention, often in the absence of central government control (Cairney 2017, 2020; Cairney and St Denny 2020). Its use would be akin to a collaborative governance mechanism, in which one potential cause of success is the process used to foster agreement rather than the intervention itself (Ansell and Gash 2008). Indeed, part of the collaboration may be to produce the rules of collective action and the criteria to evaluate of success (Ostrom 1990: 51; Ostrom et al. 2014: 285; Ostrom 2011: 16; Heikkila and Andersson 2018). A strong commitment to this process precludes the adoption of a uniform model that we might associate with narrowly defined stories of evidence-based policymaking.

Comparing Stories of Good Policymaking

These stories help us compare choices regarding how to identify and use evidence, and think of evidence-use in more-or-less decentralised policymaking systems. As Table 8.1 suggests, on initial inspection, we might expect to see a congruence between choices on evidence use *and* governance: a centralised approach to policymaking is conducive to generating evidence on uniform models of policy delivery, while a decentralised approach is conducive to deliberating and sharing stories about policy.

However, in practice, policymakers seem to try to juggle an inconsistent mix of initiatives. For example, since 'policy' is really a mix of policy instruments, a government can produce different instruments with

Table 8.1 Two stories of knowledge-informed policy analysis

	The evidence-based story	*The co-production story*
The main story	Interventions are highly regarded when backed by empirical data from international randomised control trials (RCTs).	People tell stories of policy experiences, and invite other people to learn from them. Policy is driven by governance principles based on co-producing policy with communities and users.
How should you gather evidence of policy effectiveness?	With reference to a hierarchy of evidence, with systematic reviews and RCTs at the top.	With reference to principles of good practice, and diverse sources of knowledge.
How should you 'scale up' from evidence of best practice?	Introduce the same model in each area. Require fidelity, to administer the correct dosage, and allow you to measure its effectiveness using RCTs.	Tell stories based on your experience, and invite other people to learn from them.
What aim should you prioritise?	To ensure the correct administration of the same active ingredient.	To foster key principles, such as localism and respect for communities and service user experiences.

Source: Author's own, adapted from Cairney (2017, 2020) and Cairney and Oliver (2017)

different methods of analysis. Or, more confusingly, they try to generate the best of both worlds, in which they use RCT evidence to identify an initial solution, and then encourage localism and the co-production of policy in practice (Cairney 2019, 2020).

Further, researchers often try to co-produce policy analysis by combining research with knowledge from stakeholders or service users (e.g. Crompton 2019). Bevir et al. (2019) identify several traditions of co-production on which analysts might draw, including the IAD's focus on collaborative and polycentric governance, social movements to foster 'service-user emancipation' from paternalistic public services, or Habermas-inspired ideas about deliberative democracy.

Although a collaborative approach may help ward off the inconsistent use of research by governments, it also creates major potential for confusion and inconsistency (see Flinders et al. 2016; Oliver et al. 2019; Allen et al. 2019; Clarke et al. 2019). To a large extent, these problems relate to the trade-offs at the start of this section: how many people should be involved, whose knowledge counts, who should control the process, and what is the intended outcome? Each answer involves political choice to favour one form and source of knowledge over another, and it feeds into very different notions regarding who should make policy choices based on these insights. Co-produced policy analysis costs time, money, and emotional energy, with no guarantee of any reward. Indeed, the analyst (or their client) may not like or want to incorporate what they hear, which exposes the politics that cannot be resolved by more evidence or more discussion (see Weaver 2019 on voices that challenge existing hierarchies).

Further, in some cases, the choice may be to *use the language of co-production* rather cynically, to project consensus-seeking strategies while actually seeking to get your own way (a concern expressed more profoundly by Smith 2012). If so, the long-term effect of insincere policy analytical processes may be to reduce trust in research and policy analysis (see also Oliver and Cairney 2019 on the 'instrumental' use of partnerships by researchers).

Such issues should prompt you to question your role as a policy analyst. In this chapter, we have asked if your role is simply to gather evidence for a client, or generate new insights from stakeholders and citizens. In the next chapter, we consider such questions as part of a wider examination of possible roles.

References

Allen, K., Needham, C., Hall, K., & Tanner, D. (2019). Participatory Research Meets Validated Outcome Measures: Tensions in the Co-production of Social Care Evaluation. *Social Policy & Administration, 53*(2), 311–325.

Althaus, C. (2019). Different Paradigms of Evidence and Knowledge: Recognising, Honouring, and Celebrating Indigenous Ways of Knowing and Being. *Australian Journal of Public Administration*, 1–21. https://doi.org/10.1111/1467-8500.12400.

Ansell, C., & Gash, A. (2008). Collaborative Governance in Theory and Practice. *Journal of Public Administration Research and Theory, 18*(4), 543–571.

Bevir, M., Needham, C., & Waring, J. (2019). Inside Co-production: Ruling, Resistance, and Practice. *Social Policy & Administration, 53*(2), 197–202.

Boaz, A., Davies, H., Fraser, A., & Nutley, S. (Eds.). (2019). *What Works Now?* Bristol: Policy Press.

Cairney, P. (2016). *The Politics of Evidence-based Policymaking*. London: Palgrave Pivot.

Cairney, P. (2017). Evidence-Based Best Practice Is More Political Than It Looks: A Case Study of the 'Scottish Approach'. *Evidence and Policy, 13*(3), 499–515.

Cairney, P. (2019). The UK Government's Imaginative Use of Evidence to Make Policy. *British Politics, 14*(1), 1–22.

Cairney, P. (2020). The Myth of 'evidence based policymaking' in a Decentred State. *Public Policy and Administration.* https://doi.org/10.1177/0952076720905016.

Cairney, P., & Oliver, K. (2017). Evidence-based Policymaking Is Not Like Evidence-Based Medicine, So How Far Should You Go to Bridge the Divide Between Evidence and Policy? *Health Research Policy and Systems.* https://doi.org/10.1186/s12961-017-0192-x.

Cairney, P., & St Denny, E. (2020). *Why Isn't Government Policy More Preventive?* Oxford: Oxford University Press.

Clarke, J., Waring, J., & Timmons, S. (2019). The Challenge of Inclusive Coproduction: The Importance of Situated Rituals and Emotional Inclusivity in the Coproduction of Health Research Projects. *Social Policy & Administration, 53*(2), 233–248.

Crompton, A. (2019). Inside Co-production: Stakeholder Meaning and Situated Practice. *Social Policy & Administration, 53*(2), 219–232.

Dolowitz, D., & Marsh, D. (1996). Who Learns What From Whom: A Review of the Policy Transfer Literature. *Political Studies, 44*(2), 343–357.

Dolowitz, D., & Marsh, D. (2000). Learning from Abroad: The Role of Policy Transfer in Contemporary Policy-Making. *Governance, 13*(1), 5–24.

Dunlop, C., & Radaelli, C. (2018). The Lessons of Policy Learning: Types, Triggers, Hindrances and Pathologies. *Policy & Politics, 46*(2), 255–272.

Flinders, M., Wood, M., & Cunningham, M. (2016). The Politics of Co-production: Risks, Limits and Pollution. *Evidence & Policy, 12*(2), 261–279.

Heikkila, T., & Andersson, K. (2018). Policy Design and the Added-Value of the Institutional Analysis Development Framework. *Policy and Politics, 46*(2), 309–324.

Oliver, K., & Cairney, P. (2019). The Dos and Don'ts of Influencing Policy: A Systematic Review of Advice to Academics. *Palgrave Communications, 5*(21), 1–11.

Oliver, K., Kothari, A., & Mays, N. (2019). The Dark Side of Coproduction: Do the Costs Outweigh the Benefits for Health Research? *Health Research Policy and Systems, 17*(33), 1–10. https://doi.org/10.1186/s12961-019-0432-3.

Oliver, K., & Pearce, W. (2017). Three Lessons from Evidence-based Medicine and Policy: Increase Transparency, Balance Inputs and Understand Power. *Palgrave Communications, 3*, 43. https://doi.org/10.1057/s41599-017-0045-9.

Ostrom, E. (1990). *Governing the Commons: The Evolution of Institutions for Collective Action.* Cambridge: Cambridge University Press.

Ostrom, E. (2011). Background on the Institutional Analysis and Development Framework. *Policy Studies Journal, 39*(1), 7–27.

Ostrom, E., Cox, M., & Schlager, E. (2014). An Assessment of the Institutional Analysis and Development Framework and Introduction of the Social-Ecological Systems Framework. In P. Sabatier & C. Weible (Eds.), *Theories of the Policy Process* (3rd ed.). Boulder, CO: Westview Press.

Rose, R. (1993). *Lesson-Drawing in Public Policy.* New York: Chatham House.

Rose, R. (2005). *Learning From Comparative Public Policy: A Practical Guide.* London: Routledge.

Smith, L. T. (2012). *Decolonizing Methodologies* (2nd ed.). London: Zed Books.

Weaver, B. (2019). Co-production, Governance and Practice: The Dynamics and Effects of User Voice Prison Councils. *Social Policy & Administration, 53*(2), 249–264.

CHAPTER 9

What Is Your Role as a Policy Analyst?

Abstract This chapter compares different ways to think of policy analysis as a practice and a profession. The main distinction is between the pragmatic and client-oriented role identified by most 'how to do' policy analysis texts, and the critical and decolonising role (focused on challenging inequalities and marginalisation) discussed in critical social science.

Keywords Policy analysis • Pragmatism • Critical policy analysis • Marginalised groups • Power • Decolonisation

INTRODUCTION

Our discussion so far suggests that the policy analyst role has a practical and normative element: what can you do, and what should you do? The summary of *insights from policy process research* helps us identify the limits to policy analytical and policymaker capacity. The concept of 'bounded rationality' highlights major limits on the ability of humans and organisations to process information. Humans use heuristics or cognitive shortcuts to process enough information to make choices, and institutions are the rules used by organisations to limit information processing. Terms like policymaking 'context', 'environments', and 'multi-centric policymaking' suggest that the policy process is beyond the limits of policymaker understanding and control.

In that context, policy actors need to find ways to act despite possessing incomplete information about the problem they seek to solve and the likely impact of their 'solution'. They gather information to help reduce uncertainty, but problem definition is really about exercising power to reduce ambiguity: select one way to interpret a problem (at the expense of most others), and therefore limit the relevance and feasibility of solutions. This context informs how actors might use the tools of policy analysis. Key policy analysis texts highlight the use of tools to establish technical feasibility (will it work as intended?), but policymakers also select tools for their political feasibility (who will support or oppose this measure?).

Perhaps more importantly, the summary of *insights from wider studies of power, knowledge, politics, and policy* identifies normative questions regarding whose knowledge counts and how to balance expert and deliberative forms of analytical research. Weimer and Vining (2017: 44) draw on such normative concerns to identify three main 'views on the appropriate role of the policy analyst' and assign them to views on appropriate 'analytical integrity', 'responsibility to clients', and 'adherence to one's conception of good'. In summary, an analyst can be:

1. The *objective technician*. Let analysis speak for itself, see the need for a client to remain popular as a necessary evil, and leave value choices to clients.
2. The *client's advocate*. Exploit ambiguity to further your client's position, trade loyalty to your client for access to power, and select clients who possess 'compatible value systems' and can be persuaded to change their conception of good.
3. The *issue advocate*. Highlight ambiguity when analysis does not support your aims, select the best clients for your cause, and see analysis as 'an instrument for progress towards one's conception of the good society' (compare with Pielke 2007; Jasanoff 2008).

In other words, one can pretend to be objective, focus narrowly on serving a client, or recognise that policy analysis is a political role and reflect on what is good and how to do the right thing. Further, based on our discussions so far, more detailed reflections on policy analysis may include:

1. Is your primary role to serve individual clients or some notion of the 'public good'?
2. Should you accentuate your role as an individual or as part of a wider profession?
3. Which policy analysis methods or techniques should you prioritise?
4. Who should decide how to frame problems and set the limits on the feasibility of solutions?
5. What is the balance between the potential benefits of individual 'entrepreneurship' and collective 'co-productive' processes?
6. What forms of knowledge and evidence should count in policy analysis?
7. To what extent should you gauge success in relation to the *inclusive ways in which you generate analysis* as well as the *policy impact and outcomes*.
8. What does it mean to communicate policy analysis responsibly (such as with reference to uncertainty and ambiguity)?
9. Should you provide a clear recommendation or encourage reflection and iteration?
10. Should you seek to be pragmatic or to change the world?

As such, it is possible to expect more than three types of analysts. Indeed, studies of the field—summarised in Chap. 3—suggest that (a) there are many ways to do policy analysis and (b) such roles are not necessarily mutually exclusive, since your views on their relative value could change throughout the process of analysis. You could (within reason) perform many of these roles.

POLICY ANALYSIS ARCHETYPES: PRAGMATIC AND CLIENT-ORIENTED VERSUS CRITICAL AND DECOLONISING?

To explore these issues, Cairney (2019) identifies a series of policy analyst archetypes to identify ethical ways to gather and present policy-relevant information. With the exception of entrepreneurs and systems thinkers (*the following two chapters*), most can be grouped into two main categories.

1. *The pragmatic or professional, client-oriented policy analyst*

    - Bardach (2012) provides the classic simple, workable, eight-step system to present policy analysis to policymakers while subject to time and resource-pressed political conditions.
    - Dunn (2017) also uses Wildavsky's famous phrase 'art and craft' to suggest that scientific and 'rational' methods can only take us so far.
    - Weimer and Vining (2017) provide a similar step-by-step client-focused system, but incorporating a greater focus on professional development and economic techniques (such as cost-benefit analysis) to emphasise a particular form of professional analyst.
    - Meltzer and Schwartz (2019) also focus on advice to clients, but with a greater emphasis on a wide variety of methods or techniques (including service design) to encourage the co-design of policy analysis with clients.
    - See also Smith (2015) on how to write and communicate policy analysis to clients in a political context, and Spiegelhalter (2018) and Gigerenzer (2015) on how to communicate responsibly when describing uncertainty, probability, and risk.

2. *The questioning, storytelling, or decolonising policy analyst*

    - Stone (2012) identifies the ways in which people use storytelling and argumentation techniques to define problems and justify solutions. This process is about politics and power, not objectivity and optimal solutions.
    - Bacchi (2009) analyses the wider context in which people give and use such advice, to identify the emancipatory role of analysis and encourage policy analysts to challenge dominant social constructions of problems and populations.
    - Smith (2012) shows how the 'decolonisation of research methods' can inform the generation and use of knowledge. Further, Althaus (2019) shows how to challenge dominant hierarchies of scientific knowledge to pay more respect to 'indigenous ways of knowing and being' in public administration
    - Doucet (2019) and Michener (2019) show how to apply these insights to the study of race and marginalised groups.

In other words, although each text often describes multiple roles, they generally seem clustered together into two main approaches. *Pragmatic, professional, client-orientated, and communicative* could sum up the traditional five-step approaches, while *questioning, storytelling, and decolonising* could sum up a critical challenge to narrow ways of thinking about policy analysis and the generation of policy-relevant knowledge.

Although analysts could perform multiple roles, the *emphasis* in these texts matters. Each text is setting an agenda and defining the problem of policy analysis more or less in relation to these roles. Put simply, the more you are reading about economic theory and method, the less you are reading about marginalisation and dominance.

References

Althaus, C. (2019). Different Paradigms of Evidence and Knowledge: Recognising, Honouring, and Celebrating Indigenous Ways of Knowing and Being. *Australian Journal of Public Administration*, 1–21. https://doi.org/10.1111/1467-8500.12400.

Bacchi, C. (2009). *Analysing Policy: What's the Problem Represented to Be?* NSW: Pearson.

Bardach, E. (2012). *A Practical Guide for Policy Analysis* (4th ed.). CQ Press.

Cairney, P. (2019). Policy Analysis in 750 Words: Reflecting on Your Role as a Policy Analyst. *Paul Cairney: Politics & Public Policy*, December 19. Retrieved from https://paulcairney.wordpress.com/2019/12/19/policy-analysis-in-750-words-reflecting-on-your-role-as-a-policy-analyst/.

Doucet, F. (2019). *Centering the Margins: (Re)defining Useful Research Evidence Through Critical Perspectives.* New York: William T. Grant Foundation.

Dunn, W. (2017). *Public Policy Analysis* (6th ed.). Routledge.

Gigerenzer, G. (2015). *Risk Savvy*. London: Penguin.

Jasanoff, S. (2008). Speaking Honestly to Power. *American Scientist*, 6(3), 240.

Meltzer, R., & Schwartz, A. (2019). *Policy Analysis as Problem Solving*. London: Routledge.

Michener, J. (2019). Policy Feedback in a Racialized Polity. *Policy Studies Journal*, 47(2), 423–450.

Pielke, R., Jr. (2007). *The Honest Broker: Making Sense of Science in Policy and Politics.* Cambridge: Cambridge University Press.

Smith, C. (2015). *Writing Public Policy.* Oxford University Press.

Smith, L. T. (2012). *Decolonizing Methodologies* (2nd ed.). London: Zed Books.

Spiegelhalter, D. (2018). *The Art of Statistics: Learning from Data.* London: Pelican.

Stone, D. (2012). *Policy Paradox: The Art of Political Decision Making* (3rd ed.). London: Norton.

Weimer, D., & Vining, A. (2017). *Policy Analysis: Concepts and Practice* (6th ed.). London: Routledge.

CHAPTER 10

How to Be a Policy Entrepreneur

Abstract This chapter compares different ways to think of entrepreneurship in policy analysis. The first is to identify the attributes, skills, and strategies that entrepreneurs need to succeed. The second is to qualify the success of entrepreneurship: most fail, and their success depends more on their environments than their skills.

Keywords Policy analysis • Policy entrepreneurs • Policy skills and strategies • Policymaking environments • Multiple streams analysis • Power

Introduction

One analytical role missing from the previous chapter's list is the *entrepreneurial policy analyst*. In business, an entrepreneur is an actor that makes an investment of resources, to forego short-term income in exchange for long-term financial returns. In politics, the 'return' is more difficult to describe, but political actors such as politicians or lobbyists still invest their time, energy, and money to seek a political reward. For example, Kingdon (1984: 21; 104; 165–6, summarised in Cairney 2020: 200) describes entrepreneurs as 'actors who use their knowledge of the policy process to further their own ends … with the knowledge, power, tenacity, and luck to be able to exploit windows of opportunity' for major policy change.

Major change may happen when three 'streams' (problems, policy, politics) come together at the same time: policymaker attention rises to a problem, a technically and politically feasible solution exists, and policymakers have the motive and opportunity to select it.

In that context, the idea of 'policy entrepreneurship' is important to the strategies of individual policy analysts. In particular, Mintrom (2012) highlights the benefits of 'positive thinking', creativity, deliberation, and leadership, and expands on these ideas further in 'So you want to be a policy entrepreneur?':

> *Policy entrepreneurs are energetic actors who engage in collaborative efforts in and around government to promote policy innovations. Given the enormous challenges now facing humanity, the need is great for such actors to step forward and catalyze change processes.* (Mintrom 2019: 307)

Although many entrepreneurs seem to be exceptional people, Mintrom (2019: 308-20) focuses on the *role* of entrepreneurship, built on the attributes, skills, and strategies of effective actors. Their attributes include: *ambition*, to invest resources for future reward, *social acuity*, to help anticipate how others are thinking, *credibility*, based on authority and a good track record, *sociability*, to empathise with others and form coalitions or networks, and *tenacity*, to persevere during adversity. Further, the skills that can be learned include:

- 'strategic thinking', to choose a goal and determine how to reach it
- 'team building', to recognise that policy change is a collective effort, not the responsibility of heroic individuals (compare with Mayne et al. 2018)
- 'collecting evidence', and using it 'strategically' to frame a problem and support a solution
- 'making arguments', using 'tactical argumentation' to 'win others to their cause and build coalitions of supporters' (2019: 313)
- 'engaging multiple audiences', by tailoring arguments and evidence to their beliefs and interests
- 'negotiating', such as by trading your support in this case for their support in another
- 'networking', particularly when policymaking authority is spread across multiple venues.

Finally, entrepreneurs develop strategies built on these attributes and skills:

- 'problem framing', such as to tell a story of a crisis in need of urgent attention
- 'using and expanding networks', to generate attention and support
- 'working with advocacy coalitions', to mobilise a collection of actors who already share the same beliefs
- 'leading by example', to signal commitment and allay fears about risk
- 'scaling up change processes', using policy innovation in one area to inspire wider adoption.

Overall, entrepreneurship is 'tough work' requiring 'courage', but necessary for policy disruption, by 'those who desire to make a difference, who recognize the enormous challenges now facing humanity, and the need for individuals to step forward and catalyze change' (2019: 320).

Policy Studies Qualify the Role of Entrepreneurship

The concept of entrepreneurship is also crucial to policy studies, but with a tendency to compare stories of exceptional *individuals* with stories of their policymaking *environments*. The literature is huge (see Cairney 2018 for a list of further reading), but a general take-home message is: (a) recognise the value of entrepreneurship, and invest in relevant skills and strategies, *but* (b) do not overstate its likely impact, and (c) note the unequal access to political resources associated with entrepreneurs. For example, Cairney (2018) draws on multiple streams analysis to describe 'three habits of successful policy entrepreneurs':

1. *Don't focus on bombarding policymakers with evidence.* Instead, entrepreneurs tell a good story, grab the audience's interest, and the audience demands information.
2. *By the time people pay attention to a problem it's too late to produce a solution.* Entrepreneurs have a technically and politically feasible solution ready to attach to problems.
3. *When your environment changes, your strategy changes.* Entrepreneurs may have limited direct influence in large and crowded political systems, but more impact in smaller and less competitive venues.

This basic message can be expanded as follows.

Most Entrepreneurs Fail
It is common to relate entrepreneurship to stories of exceptional *individuals* and invite people to learn from their success. However, the logical conclusion is that success is exceptional and most policy actors will fail. Mintrom's focus on key *skills* takes us away from this reliance on exceptional actors, and ties in with other policy studies-informed advice on how to make an impact with evidence (see Chap. 12, and Stoker 2010; Weible et al. 2012). However, it is possible to invest a huge amount of time and effort in entrepreneurial skills without any of that investment paying off (Cairney 2020: 104). Entrepreneurs can adopt the same basic strategies, and some will succeed while others will fail (Jarvis and He 2020).

Even if Entrepreneurs Succeed, the Explanation Comes More from Their Environments than Their Individual Skills
Think of individual entrepreneurship and the policymaking environment as on two sides of the same coin of explanation. Then imagine that the coin is rigged to land on the environment almost every time. Many policy studies, including by Kingdon, rely heavily on evolutionary metaphors (Cairney 2013). As such, while entrepreneurs are the actors most equipped to thrive within their environments, their environment set the parameters in which they can succeed (Room 2016). Indeed, when describing politics at the US federal level, Kingdon uses the additional metaphor of 'surfers waiting for the big wave'. Entrepreneurs may be more influential at a more local scale, but the evidence of their success (independent of the conditions in which they operate) is not overwhelming. So, self-aware entrepreneurs think more about how to 'surf the waves' than controlling the sea (Cairney and Jones 2016).

This insight helps us make a profound distinction between two different conceptions of a 'window of opportunity'. The first is an opportunity for an individual to influence an individual when they are in the right frame of mind (according to the 'emotional state of the audience'). The second is to exploit the right moment during a 'series of events in political systems' (Cairney and Kwiatkowski 2017: 5). The former could be possible in an informal meeting or achieved with a well-worded client-oriented report. However, the latter is much more complicated, since we may be unsure about who the audience should be, far less having a direct route to influence. Policy research shows that the key actors are not necessarily at the 'centre' or the actors in formal positions of power. Further, most actors ignore most issues most of the time, and our analysis may be more geared towards encouraging attention from a particular audience, rather than assuming that all audiences will be interested. Perhaps most importantly, Kingdon (1984: 122–36) seems to suggest that the 'evolution' of an idea towards feasibility can take anything from 'a while' to 'a few years' to '25 years'! The latter puts a very different spin on the impact of entrepreneurial policy analysis.

Inequalities of Power Cause Inequalities in Successful Entrepreneurship
Many studies of entrepreneurs highlight the stories of tenacious individuals with limited resources but the burning desire to make a difference. The alternative story is that most entrepreneurs have advantages because political resources are distributed profoundly unequally. Few people have the resources to: run for elected office; attend elite universities, or find other ways to develop the kinds of personal networks that often relate to social background; develop the credibility built on a track record in a position of authority (such as in government or science); be in the position to invest resources now, to secure future gains; or be in an influential position to exploit windows of opportunity.

Therefore, when focusing on entrepreneurial policy analysis, we should encourage the development of a suite of useful skills, but not expect equal access to that development or the same payoff from entrepreneurial action. As Chap. 12 discusses, we can use policy theories to explore how far we would go to make an impact as individuals, but should not confuse this focus on individuals with the assumption of equal opportunities for each individual.

References

Cairney, P. (2013). What is Evolutionary Theory and How Does it Inform Policy Studies? *Policy and Politics, 41*(2), 279–298.
Cairney, P. (2018). Three Habits of Successful Policy Entrepreneurs. *Policy and Politics, 46*(2), 199–217.
Cairney, P. (2020). *Understanding Public Policy* (2nd ed.). London: Red Globe.
Cairney, P., & Jones, M. (2016). Kingdon's Multiple Streams Approach: What Is the Empirical Impact of This Universal Theory? *Policy Studies Journal, 44*(1), 37–58.

Cairney, P. and Kwiatkowski, R. (2017). How to Communicate Effectively with Policymakers: Combine Insights from Psychology and Policy Studies. *Palgrave Communications*, 3, 37. https://www.nature.com/articles/s41599-017-0046-8.

Jarvis, D. S., & He, A. J. (2020). Policy Entrepreneurship and Intuitional Change: Who, How, and why? *Public Administration and Development*, 40(1), 3–10.

Kingdon, J. (1984). *Agendas, Alternatives and Public Policies.* New York, NY: Harper Collins.

Mayne, R., Green, D., Guijt, I., Walsh, M., English, R., & Cairney, P. (2018). Using Evidence to Influence Policy: Oxfam's Experience. *Palgrave Communications*, 4(122), 1–10. https://doi.org/10.1057/s41599-018-0176-7.

Mintrom, M. (2012). *Contemporary Policy Analysis.* Oxford: Oxford University Press.

Mintrom, M. (2019). So you want to be a policy entrepreneur? *Policy Design and Practice*, 2(4), 307–323. https://doi.org/10.1080/25741292.2019.1675989.

Room, G. (2016). *Agile Actors on Complex Terrains: Transformative Realism and Public Policy.* London: Routledge.

Stoker, G. (2010). Translating Experiments into Policy. *The ANNALS of the American Academy of Political and Social Science*, 628(1), 47–58.

Weible, C., Heikkila, T., deLeon, P., & Sabatier, P. (2012). Understanding and Influencing the Policy Process. *Policy Sciences*, 45(1), 1–21.

CHAPTER 11

Policy Analysis as Systems Thinking

Abstract This chapter compares different ways to think about systems thinking in policy analysis. Some focus on systems thinking to avoid the unintended consequences of too-narrow definitions of problems and processes: if we engage in systems thinking effectively, we can understand systems well enough to control, manage, or influence them. Others suggest that policy emerges from complex systems in the absence of central government control. Therefore, we need to acknowledge these limitations properly, to accept our limitations, and avoid the mechanistic language of 'policy levers' which exaggerate human or government control.

Keywords Policy analysis • Complex systems • Systems thinking • Policy mixes • Socio-ecological systems • Socio-technical systems

Introduction

The idea of 'systems thinking' is potentially useful to policy analysis, particularly if it takes us away from a tendency to see the world through entrepreneurs, or individual analysts and clients. However, there are 101 ways to describe systems, which puts them at risk of meaning everything

Table 11.1 Ten stories of systems thinking

Application of complex/system language	Systems thinking is about ...
Complex system	Learning and adapting to the limits to policymaker control
Complex policy problems	Addressing policy problems holistically
Complex policy mixes	Anticipating the effect of a new policy instrument
Socio-technical systems	Identifying the role of new technologies, protected initially in a niche, and fostered by a supportive environment
Socio-ecological systems	Identifying how actors make rules to foster trust and cooperation
The metaphor of systems	Projecting the sense that policy is complicated, but governments can still look like they are in control
Order from chaos	The ability to turn potential chaos into well-managed systems
Disproportionate impact	Using a small shift in a system to produce profound change
Thinking about ourselves	The humility to accept our limited knowledge of the world
Rethink cause-and-effect	Rethinking policy-relevant research on social behaviour

Source: author's own

and therefore nothing (compare with Wildavsky 1973; Hogwood 1986). Systems thinking can be useful to policy analysis, but only if we can (a) clarify its meaning when described by multiple approaches, and (b) incorporate insights from policy studies, to (c) establish if systems thinking implies high versus low policymaker control over a policymaking system.

To that end, please bear in mind two overall stories of systems thinking as we explore ten examples in the field (summarised in Table 11.1):

1. *Systems thinking in policy analysis.* A focus on systems helps us avoid the unintended consequences of too-narrow definitions of problems and processes (systems thinking, not simplistic thinking). Further, if we engage in systems thinking effectively, we can understand systems well enough to control, manage, or influence them.
2. *The study of complex policymaking systems.* Policy studies employing the language of complex systems suggest that policy *emerges* from complex systems in the absence of central government control. Therefore, we need to acknowledge these limitations properly, to accept our limitations, and avoid the mechanistic language of 'policy levers' which exaggerate human or government control.

Ten Stories of Complex Systems

This section identifies many possible meanings of complex system and relates them to simple systems thinking storylines. For example, from this book so far, we can already identify the first three different meanings of complex or complex system (examples 1–3), and each presents different implications for systems thinking.

1. *Complex policymaking systems.* Complexity theory suggests that systems cannot be reduced to individual action, can cause the same action to have disproportionate effects, exhibit path dependence and regularities of behaviour interrupted by short bursts of change, and exhibit 'emergence', or behaviour that results from the interaction between elements at a local level rather than central direction (Cairney 2012, 2020; Geyer and Cairney 2015). Therefore, avoid 'single-shot' policy analysis in which there is a one-size-fits-all policy solution, use trial-and-error and give local actors the freedom to adapt rather than seeking central government order, and rethink the ways in which we think about government 'failure' (Geyer 2012; Hallsworth 2011) (see Chap. 4).

- Systems thinking is about learning and adapting to the limits to policymaker control.

2. *Complex policy problems.* Dunn (2017: 73) describes the interdependent nature of problems:

> Subjectively experienced problems—crime, poverty, unemployment, inflation, energy, pollution, health, security—cannot be decomposed into independent subsets without running the risk of producing an approximately right solution to the wrong problem. A key characteristic of systems of problems is that the whole is greater—that is, qualitatively different—than the simple sum of its parts.

- Systems thinking is about addressing policy problems holistically.

3. *Complex policy mixes.* 'Policy' is actually a collection of policy instruments. Although Lindblom famously described their incremental accumulation, their overall effect may be 'non-linear' (Spyridaki and Flamos 2014), difficult to predict, and subject to emergent outcomes. This point is crucial to policy analysis: does the proposal of a new policy instrument

necessitate a rethink of all instruments, to anticipate the effect of policy change? (See Chap. 7, 'Producing Solutions as Part of a Policy Mix'.)

- Systems thinking is about anticipating the disproportionate effect of a new policy instrument.

Munro and Cairney's (2020) systematic review of the literature on 'energy systems' and 'whole systems thinking' helps identify additional ways in which researchers and policymakers make sense of systems (examples 4–7).

4. *Socio-technical systems*. Possibly the most established approach in this field is the 'multi-level perspective' (MLP) developed by Geels and colleagues (e.g. Geels 2002, 2004; Rogge et al. 2020). They use it to help explain, predict, or encourage the transition from unsustainable to sustainable energy systems with reference to three concepts (Chilvers et al. 2017: 442). The *macro-landscape* represents the 'broader political, social and cultural values and institutions that form the deep structural relationships of a society and only change slowly'. The *socio-technical regime* is the 'prevailing set of routines or practices' that may be conducive to 'generating incremental innovation'. *Niche innovation* describes the development of new, game-changing, sustainable technologies in places that encourage learning and innovation and protect the technology initially from the market conditions and other unfavourable conditions often associated with the other levels.

- Systems thinking is about identifying new technologies, developed and protected initially in a 'niche', while engaging with a more or less supportive 'social and political environment'. It is often used to identify what it would take to produce a radical energy system transformation and the political factors that undermine it (see also Chap. 7).

5. *Socio-ecological systems* (SES). Munro and Cairney (2020) explore the ways in which energy systems thinkers could learn from the Institutional Analysis and Development Framework. In particular, energy systems studies tend to downplay (or misunderstand) the role for government in system change and accentuate the need for cooperation between a large number of non-governmental actors 'to manage finite resources and minimise environmental damage' (2020: 7). In that context, Ostrom's (2009)

conception of SES helps identify how actors might develop the 'rules and mechanisms to ensure high cooperation among many actors and societal ownership of the means to achieve energy transitions' (Munro and Cairney 2020: 7).

- Systems thinking is about identifying the conditions under which actors develop layers of rules to foster trust and cooperation (see Chap. 8, 'A Story of Co-production in Policymaking').

6. *The metaphor of systems.* However, it is usually difficult to find evidence that policymakers or governments refer to these approaches when describing systems. Rather, Munro and Cairney (2020) find that the UK and Scottish government use the language of systems loosely and metaphorically to indicate an awareness of the interconnectedness of things in energy (compare with Adams 1988). As such, they can describe a set of *complicated* relationships while trying to project the sense that policy problems are amenable to central government influence.

- Systems thinking is about projecting the sense that (a) policy and policymaking are complicated, but (b) governments can still look like they are influential.

7. *The old way of establishing order from chaos.* Policymakers and researchers do not go so far as to assert central government control. It is increasingly rare to invoke the (now-diminished) faith in science and rational management techniques to control the natural world for human benefit. Rather, these ways of thinking tend to be historical reference points, akin to the policy studies focus on cycles and rationality (see Hughes 1983, 2004; Hughes and Hughes 2000; and Checkland 1999 on 'hard' versus 'soft' systems approaches).

- Systems thinking *was* about the human ability to turn potential chaos into well-managed systems (such as 'large technical systems' to distribute energy)

8. *The new way of accepting complexity but seeking to make an impact.* Still, many systems thinkers have not given up on the idea that we can produce a disproportionate impact on systems if we understand them well. For example, Meadows' (1999) influential work on issues such as

environmental sustainability argues that we can identify 'leverage points', or the places that help us 'intervene in a system' (compare with Arnold and Wade 2015 on education).

- Systems thinking is about the human ability to use a small shift in a system to produce profound changes in that system.

9. *A way of thinking about ourselves.* At the other end of the spectrum, we find accounts that use the language of complexity to identify and embrace the limits to human cognition, and accept that all human understandings of complex systems are limited to a small number of perspectives.

- Systems thinking is about developing the 'wisdom' and 'humility' to accept our limited knowledge of the world (Firth 2017).

10. *A way to rethink cause-and-effect.* Our final relevant account suggests that policy analysis should not follow the lead of current research methods, which are too narrowly focused on the idea of linear cause-and-effect. Rather, social systems exhibit emergent properties that are not amenable to simple interpretation or intervention. For example, Rutter et al. (2017) identify the need for new forms of research to analyse the potentially non-linear effect of public health interventions.

- Systems thinking is about rethinking the ways in which governments, funders, or researchers conduct policy-relevant research on social behaviour.

How Can We Clarify Systems Thinking and Use It Effectively in Policy Analysis?

Imagine that you are in a room of self-styled systems thinkers, trying to establish what you all mean by systems thinking. First, there may be some encouragement to Craven (2019), who still 'believes in the power of systems thinking'. Some of these ten discussions seem to complement each other. For example, we can use 3 *and* 10 to reject a narrow idea of 'evidence-based policymaking', in which the focus is on (a) using experimental methods to establish cause-and-effect in relation to one policy instrument, without showing (b) the overall impact on policy and outcomes (Cairney 2016; see Chap. 8, *A story of 'evidence-based policymaking'*). Further, 1–3 might connect to 9 as part of a general story on the need for policy analyst humility when seeking to understand and influence complex policy problems, solutions, and policymaking systems. In other words, you could define systems thinking in relation to the need to rethink the ways in which we understand—and try to address—policy problems.

Second, however, there are clearly key tensions among the list of ten stories. Some are about intervening to take control of systems or, at least, make a disproportionate difference from a small change. Others are about accepting our inability to understand, far less manage, these systems. Some are about managing *policymaking* systems, and others about *social* systems (or systems of *policy problems*), without making a clear connection between each endeavour. For example, it is not unusual to find approaches on rethinking societal cause-and-effect (approach 10), connected to (a) a high researcher confidence in our ability to intervene (approach 7 or 8) *but also* (b) metaphorical governmental strategies (approach 6).

In that context, note that too much collective effort goes into (a) restating, over and over and over again, the potential benefits of systems thinking, leaving almost no time for (b) clarifying systems thinking well enough to move on to these profound differences in thinking. It may be a useful approach to policy analysis, but only if you and your audience are clear on what you mean, how you use systems thinking to identify problems, and what you think about the limits to government action.

References

Adams, D. (1988). *Dirk Gently's Holistic Detective Agency*. London: Pan Books.
Arnold, R., & Wade, J. (2015). A Definition of Systems Thinking: A Systems Approach. *Procedia Computer Science, 44*, 669–678.
Cairney, P. (2012). Complexity Theory in Political Science and Public Policy. *Political Studies Review, 10*(3), 346–358.
Cairney, P. (2016). *The Politics of Evidence-based Policymaking*. London: Palgrave Pivot.
Cairney, P. (2020). *Understanding Public Policy* (2nd ed.). London: Red Globe.
Checkland, P. (1999). Systems Thinking. In W. Currie & B. Galliers (Eds.), *Rethinking Management Information Systems* (pp. 45–56). Oxford: Oxford University Press.
Chilvers, J., Foxon, T., Galloway, S., Hammond, G., Infield, D., Leach, M., Pearson, P., Strachan, N., Strbac, G., & Thomson, M. (2017). Realising Transition Pathways for a More Electric, Low-Carbon Energy System in the

United Kingdom: Challenges, Insights and Opportunities. *Proceedings of the Institution of Mechanical Engineers, Part A: Journal of Power and Energy, 231*(6), 440–477.

Craven, L. (2019, December 19). Do We Need a Theory of Change for Systems Change? *LinkedIn Pulse*. Retrieved from https://www.linkedin.com/pulse/do-we-need-theory-change-systems-luke-craven/.

Dunn, W. (2017). *Public Policy Analysis* (6th ed.). London: Routledge.

Firth, S. (2017, September 17). Making Sense of Complexity. *Human Parts*. Retrieved from https://humanparts.medium.com/making-sense-of-complexity-ee78755d56b9.

Geels, F. (2002). Technological Transitions as Evolutionary Reconfiguration Processes: A Multi-Level Perspective and a Case-Study. *Research Policy, 31*(8-9), 1257–1274.

Geels, F. (2004). From Sectoral Systems of Innovation to Socio-Technical Systems: Insights About Dynamics and Change from Sociology and Institutional Theory. *Research Policy, 33*(6-7), 897–920.

Geyer, R. (2012). Can Complexity Move UK Policy Beyond "Evidence-Based Policy Making" and the "Audit Culture"? *Political Studies, 60*(1), 20–43.

Geyer, R., & Cairney, P. (Eds.). (2015). *Handbook on Complexity and Public Policy*. Cheltenham: Edward Elgar.

Hallsworth, M. (2011). *System Stewardship: The Future of Policymaking*. London: Institute for Government.

Hogwood, B. (1986). If Consultation Is Everything, Then Maybe It's Nothing. *Strathclyde Papers on Government and Politics*, 44 (Glasgow: University of Strathclyde).

Hughes, T. (1983). *Networks of Power*. London: The Johns Hopkins University Press.

Hughes, T. (2004). *Human Built World: How to Think About Technology and Culture*. Chicago: University of Chicago Press.

Hughes, T., & Hughes, A. (2000). Introduction. In A. Hughes & T. Hughes (Eds.), *Systems, Experts, and Computers* (pp. 1–26). London: MIT Press.

Meadows, D. (1999). *Leverage Points*. Hartland, VT: The Sustainability Institute.

Munro, F., & Cairney, P. (2020). A Systematic Review of Energy Systems: The Role of Policymaking in Sustainable Transitions. *Renewable & Sustainable Energy Reviews, 119*, 1–10.

Ostrom, E. (2009). A General Framework for Analyzing Sustainability of Social-Ecological Systems. *Science, 325*(5939), 419–422.

Rogge, K., Pfluger, B., & Geels, F. (2020). Transformative Policy Mixes in Socio-Technical Scenarios: The Case of the Low-Carbon Transition of the German Electricity System (2010–2050). *Technological Forecasting and Social Change, 119259*, 1–15. https://doi.org/10.1016/j.techfore.2018.04.002.

Rutter, H., Savona, N., Glonti, K., Bibby, J., Cummins, S., Finegood, D. T., Greaves, F., Harper, L., Hawe, P., Moore, L., & Petticrew, M. (2017). The Need for a Complex Systems Model of Evidence for Public Health. *The Lancet, 390*(10112), 2602–2604.

Spyridaki, N. A., & Flamos, A. (2014). A Paper Trail of Evaluation Approaches to Energy and Climate Policy Interactions. *Renewable and Sustainable Energy Reviews, 40*, 1090–1107.

Wildavsky, A. (1973). If Planning Is Everything, Maybe It's Nothing. *Policy Sciences, 4*(2), 127–153.

CHAPTER 12

How Much Impact Can You Expect from Your Analysis?

Abstract This chapter argues that policy analysts cannot expect to influence policymakers routinely, even if they follow 'how to do policy analysis' texts to the letter. It explores the extent to which analysts should go further to secure their proposed policy solutions, drawing on policy theories to identify a 'ladder of ethical engagement'. Safe options include to find ways to navigate policymaking systems and tell stories to appeal to the beliefs of your audience. More challenging options include to support your allies and demonise opponents, exploit low attention to most issues, and reinforce the objectionable beliefs of your clients.

Keywords Policy analysis • Ethical policy analysis • Research impact • Policy narratives • Advocacy coalitions • Social construction of target populations

INTRODUCTION

These discussions of entrepreneurs and systems thinkers are potentially useful, but only if informed by wider studies of politics and policymaking. To demonstrate, let's return to Radin's (2019) account of a major shift in the impact that policy analysts can expect from their reports. Gone are the days of a centralised process containing a small number of analysts, inside government, giving technical advice about policy formulation, on the assumption that policy problems would be solved via analysis and action. In their place, Radin (2019) describes more competition, more analysts spread across and outside government, with a less obvious audience, and—even if there is a client—high uncertainty about where the analysis fits into the bigger picture. Entrepreneurs and systems thinkers could respond well, but their effectiveness relates primarily to their context.

The old image of policy analysis signalled an expectation for high impact that we could not reasonably expect any more: policy analysts faced low competition, a clearly defined and powerful audience, and their analysis was expected to feed directly into choice. Yet, the impetus to seek high and direct impact remains, and it helps explain a lot of the pragmatic forms of policy analysis described in five-step texts, including: tailor your analysis to your audience; anticipate your client's beliefs, motivation, and needs; tell a good story; communicate with clarity and brevity; and use evidence that is policy-relevant and identify politically feasible solutions.

While many of these recommendations are familiar to scientists and researchers, they generally have far lower expectations about their likely impact, particularly if those expectations are informed by policy studies (Cairney and Oliver 2018; Oliver and Cairney 2019). In that context, Weiss' (1976, 1977a, b, 1979) work is a key reference point. It gives us a menu of ways in which policymakers might use research evidence:

- to inform solutions to a problem identified by policymakers
- as one of many sources of information used by policymakers, alongside 'stakeholder' advice and professional and service user experience
- as a resource used selectively by politicians, with entrenched positions, to bolster their case
- as a tool of government, to show it is acting (by funding research), or to measure how well policy is working
- as a source of 'enlightenment', shaping how people think over the long term.

Analysts such as researchers may have a role, but they struggle (a) to find the right time to act and (b) to get attention when competing with many other policy actors. In other words, their audience and environment are more important to an explanation of policy analysis success. The demand for information from policy analysts may be disproportionately high when policymakers pay attention to a problem and disproportionately low when they feel that they have addressed it. A lot of routine, continuous, impact tends to occur out of the public spotlight, based on rules and expectations that most policy actors take for granted. Further, the usual advice to policy analysts and researchers *may* look very similar: keep it concise, tailor it to your audience, make evidence 'policy-relevant', and give advice (don't sit on the fence). However, unless researchers are prepared to act quickly, to gather data *efficiently* (not *comprehensively*), to meet a tight brief for a client, they are not really in the impact business described by most policy analysis texts.

How Far Would You Go to Secure Impact from Your Analysis?

Given all we have discussed so far, the phrase 'speak truth to power' may seem to provide a misleading rallying cry for policy analysts. It suggests that they can identify a small group of powerful people at the 'centre' of government, and use the best evidence to persuade them of the truth about a policy problem and its solution. Rather, the truth is disputed and the locus of power is elusive. In other words, the interpretation of policy problems is contested, and power may be held by far more people spread across many policymaking 'centres'.

These insights help explain why so much policy advice is pragmatic and client-oriented. Further, that analysis seems sensible for policy analysts who seek a successful and long-term professional career, and is based on simple heuristics based on the psychology of communication:

> This involves showing simple respect and seeking ways to secure their trust, rather than feeling egotistically pleased about 'speaking truth to power' without discernible progress. Effective engagement requires preparation, diplomacy, and good judgement as much as good evidence. (Cairney and Kwiatkowski 2017: 2)

However, it is less helpful for other actors. For example, researchers bemoaning the evidence-policy gap seek more rapid and effective ways to close it (Cairney 2016). Further, many policy analysts, who recognise the emancipatory role of research, seek to challenge dominant ways of thinking and major inequalities and marginalisation among some social groups. For such actors, pragmatism may be more associated with a defence of the status quo than effective action.

In that context, we should note that policy studies can be useful but they seek primarily to describe and explain policy processes, which does not translate directly into advice on how to respond effectively. Rather, they help us identify and think about ever-present dilemmas about the line that researchers and analysts feel they should draw when they seek to engage politically as a means to an end.

The Ladder of Ethical Engagement

I describe this thought experiment as a *ladder of ethical engagement* to prompt you to decide how far you should go, from telling a simple story to mobilise your audience, to only engaging with allies, limiting debate to privilege (say) expert opinion, and framing the evidence to be most consistent with the questionable beliefs of politicians. This discussion helps analysts identify what they would do when they accept that policy problems will never be solved simply with better communication. Further, in live presentations, I use Hieronymus Bosch's *The Garden of Earthly Delights*, which contains a picture of a ladder going up into someone's rear end, to visualise this ascent into the world of inescapable political trade-offs.

First, let us begin on the safe grassy terrain at the bottom of the ladder, summed up by the 'how to be effective' advice that you might get by combining (a) policy analysis and (b) the policy theory insights summarised in Fig. 4.2, p. 54 (see also Cairney and Oliver 2018), including:

- *Find the right actors.* If there are so many potential authoritative venues, devote considerable energy to finding where the 'action' is.
- *Study institutions.* Even if you find the right venue, you will not know the unwritten rules unless you study them intensely.
- *Access networks.* Some networks are close-knit and difficult to access because bureaucracies have operating procedures that favour some sources of evidence. Actors can be privileged insiders in some venues and excluded completely in others.
- *Relate your ideas to existing paradigms.* If your evidence challenges an existing paradigm, you need a persuasion strategy good enough to prompt a shift of attention to a policy problem and a willingness to understand that problem in a new way.
- *Exploit events and opportunities.* You can try to find the right time to use evidence to exploit a crisis leading to major policy change, but the opportunities are few and chances of success low.

In that context, theory-informed studies recommend investing your time over the long term—to build alliances, trust in the messenger, knowledge of the system, and to seek 'windows of opportunity' for policy change—but offer no assurances that any of this investment will ever pay off. More specific theories can help us identify what to try next. However, a simple heuristic is that the ethical dilemmas increase in intensity in line with your attempt to be effective in a highly political policymaking environment, particularly for analysts who see their role as to be objective (see Cairney et al. 2018).

Step 1: Change Levels of Attention to Issues, Not Minds
The narrative policy framework (NPF) suggests that narratives can produce a measurable policy impact, but primarily to reinforce the beliefs of policy actors. The existing beliefs of the audience often seem more important than the skills of the storyteller. Therefore, to maximise the impact of evidence, (a) tell a story which appeals to the biases of your audiences and (b) employ Riker's (1986) 'heresthetic' strategies to increase the salience of one belief at the expense of another rather than ask someone to change their belief entirely (Crow and Jones 2018).

Step 2: Engage Only with Actors Who Share Your Beliefs
The advocacy coalition framework (ACF) suggests that actors enter politics to turn their beliefs into policy. In highly salient issues, coalition actors romanticise their own cause and demonise their opponents. This competition extends to the use of evidence: each coalition may demand different evidence, or interpret the same evidence differently, to support their own cause. One coalition may accept your analysis while another rejects it wholeheartedly. Your analysis may be an easy sell to one audience but a futile exercise to another. If so, the most feasible strategy may be to treat evidence as a resource to support the coalitions which support your cause, and to engage minimally with competitor coalitions who seek to ignore or discredit your evidence. Only in less salient issues will we find a 'brokerage' role for analysts or scientists (Weible and Ingold 2018).

Step 3: Exercise Power to Limit Debate and Dominate Policymaker Attention
Punctuated equilibrium theory (PET) identifies the role of 'disproportionate information processing' (Baumgartner et al. 2018). Policymakers can only pay attention to a small number of issues and must ignore the

rest. High levels of attention may contribute to major policy change, while minimal attention may contribute to minor change. Many researchers would respond by seeking the highest possible attention for their issue, to encourage debate and exhort policymakers to do the right thing, given the evidence. However, step 3 takes a different direction, based on the idea that there is better value from low attention. PET studies show how policy actors frame issues to limit external attention. If they can define a problem successfully as *solved*, with only the technical details relating to regulation and implementation to be addressed, they can help reduce external attention and privilege the demand for evidence from analysts and scientific experts. In other words, they would be building on insights from studies of 'policy communities' (relationships between policymakers and influencers) built on following the 'rules of the game' to help insulate their deliberations and choices from external scrutiny (Jordan and Maloney 1997; Jordan and Cairney 2013).

Step 4. Frame Evidence to Be Consistent with Objectionable Beliefs
Social construction and policy design theory (SCPD) suggests that, when dealing with salient issues, policymakers exploit social stereotypes strategically, or rely on their emotions, to define target populations as deserving of government benefits or punishments (Schneider et al. 2014). Some populations can challenge (or exploit the rewards of) their image, but many are powerless to respond. Many social groups become disenchanted with politics because they are punished by government policy and excluded from debate. To find an influential audience for evidence, one may be most effective by framing analysis evidence to be sympathetic to such stereotype-led political strategies.

The main role of these discussions is to expose the assumptions that we make about the primacy of evidence-informed policy analysis and the lengths to which we are willing to go to privilege its use. Policy studies suggest that the most effective ways to privilege research evidence may be to: manipulate the order in which we consider issues and make choices; refuse to engage in debate with our competitors; and frame issues to minimise attention or maximise the convergence between evidence and the rhetorical devices of cynical politicians. As such, they expose stark ethical dilemmas regarding the consequences for democracy. Put simply, the most effective evidence advocacy strategies may be inconsistent with wider democratic principles and key initiatives such as participatory policymaking.

If so, these discussions prompt us to consider the ways in which we can value research evidence up to a certain point, and to produce more 'co-productive' strategies which rebalance efforts to limit participation (to privilege expertise) and encourage it (to privilege deliberative and participatory forms of democracy). This approach is more honest and realistic than the more common story that science and scientific policy analysis is, by its very nature, the antidote to populist or dysfunctional politics.

REFERENCES

Baumgartner, F., Jones, B., & Mortensen, P. (2018). Punctuated Equilibrium Theory. In C. Weible & P. Sabatier (Eds.), *Theories of the Policy Process* (4th ed.). Chicago: Westview.

Cairney, P. (2016). *The Politics of Evidence-based Policymaking*. London: Palgrave Pivot.

Cairney, P. and Kwiatkowski, R. (2017). How to Communicate Effectively with Policymakers: Combine Insights from Psychology and Policy Studies. *Palgrave Communications*, 3, 37. https://www.nature.com/articles/s41599-017-0046-8.

Cairney, P., & Oliver, K. (2018). How Should Academics Engage in Policymaking to Achieve Impact? *Political Studies Review*. https://doi.org/10.1177/1478929918807714.

Cairney, P., Oliver, K., De Feo, A., Gain, V., Marra, M., Marvulli, L. Moynihan, D., & Renn, O. (2018, December 3). *Report by the Public Policy, Administration and Sociology Group*. To the European Commission Joint Research Centre). Retrieved from https://paulcairney.files.wordpress.com/2019/08/cairney-et-al-enlightenment-jrc-report-final-3.12.18.pdf.

Crow, D., & Jones, M. (2018). Narratives as Tools for Influencing Policy Change. *Policy & Politics*, 46(2), 217–234.

Jordan, A. G., & Cairney, P. (2013). What is the "Dominant Model" of British Policy Making? Comparing Majoritarian and Policy Community Ideas. *British Politics*, 8(3), 233–259.

Jordan, A. G., & Maloney, W. A. (1997). Accounting for Subgovernments: Explaining the Persistence of Policy Communities. *Administration and Society*, 29(5), 557–583.

Oliver, K., & Cairney, P. (2019). The Dos and Don'ts of Influencing Policy: A Systematic Review of Advice to Academics. *Palgrave Communications*, 5(21), 1–11.

Radin, B. (2019). *Policy Analysis in the Twenty-First Century*. London: Routledge.

Riker, W. (1986). *The Art of Political Manipulation*. New Haven: Yale University Press.

Schneider, A., Ingram, H., & deLeon, P. (2014). Democratic Policy Design: Social Construction of Target Populations. In P. Sabatier & C. Weible (Eds.), *Theories of the Policy Process*. Boulder: Westview Press.

Weible, C., & Ingold, K. (2018). Why Advocacy Coalitions Matter and Practical Insights About Them. *Policy & Politics, 46*(2), 325–343.

Weiss, C. (1976). Using Social Science for Social Policy. *Policy Studies Journal, 4*(3), 234–238.

Weiss, C. (1977a). Research for Policy's Sake: The Enlightenment Function of Social Research. *Policy Analysis, 3*, 531–545.

Weiss, C. (1977b). *Using Social Research in Public Policy-Making*. Lexington: D. C. Heath.

Weiss, C. (1979). The many meanings of research utilization. *Public Administration Review, 39*(5), 426–431.

CHAPTER 13

Conclusion: Combining Insights on Policy Analysis

Abstract This chapter concludes by comparing—and seeking to combine—three different ways to understand policy analysis. Classic guides provide a five-step plan to identify a problem and recommend solutions. Policy process research identifies the ways in which policymaking environments constrain and facilitate action. Critical policy analysis shows how to incorporate a commitment to challenging inequalities of power and the marginalisation of social groups.

Keywords Policy analysis • Policy process research • Critical policy analysis • Values • Co-production • Politics of knowledge

INTRODUCTION

In the preface, I argue that classic policy analysis could improve in two main ways. First, draw more on policy process research to see policy analysis as part of a bigger picture over which individuals have limited knowledge and even less control. Second, give more attention to studies of power and inequalities in politics to explore the role of policy analysis in (a) dismissing important claims to knowledge among marginalised groups and (b) contributing to 'solutions' that cause a disproportionately negative impact on the lives of marginalised populations. In other words, this is hopefully a conversation between three participants: policy analysis, policy process, and critical social science accounts. Stone sums up the possibilities for such a conversation:

> Whether you are a policy analyst, a policy researcher, a policy advocate, a policy maker, or an engaged citizen, my hope for Policy Paradox is that it helps you to go beyond your job description and the tasks you are given—to think hard about your own core values, to deliberate with others, and to make the world a better place. (Stone 2012: 13)

One legitimate obstacle to this conversation is the constraint usually associated with the policy analyst's task: they need to report to a client. As such, it may be possible to find the insights in this book interesting but not actionable. Pragmatism is the order of the day. Or, perhaps policymakers tend to commission policy analysis from individuals and organisations that already share their beliefs, or have a track record based on following the rules of the game. In which case, perhaps no one will find it desirable to examine a wider process of challenging a client's assumptions.

On the other hand, many insights from policy process research suggest that five-step analyses may be pragmatic in one sense (they get the job done) but not another (they do not have an actual impact on policy and policymaking). As such, reflection on these insights may be part of a policy analysis strategy to maximise effectiveness. Awareness of the policymaking environment is indispensable to effective policy analysis.

What Do Policy Analysts Need to Learn About Policymaking?

The first lesson is to pay serious attention to bounded rationality and policymaker psychology. People engage emotionally with information. Any advice to keep analysis concise is incomplete without a focus on framing and persuasion. Simplicity helps reduce cognitive load, while framing helps present the information in relation to the beliefs of your audience. If so, to pretend to be an objective policy analyst is a cop-out. To provide long, rigorous, and meticulous reports that few people read is futile. Instead, tell a convincing story with a clear moral, or frame policy analysis to grab your audience's attention and generate enthusiasm to solve a problem. As Stone (2012: 11) puts it, five-step policy analysis (identify objectives, identify alternatives, predict their effects, evaluate alternatives, choose) is pervasive, but it 'ignores our emotional feelings and moral intuitions' (2012: 11).

The second lesson is to adapt to policymaking complexity. Policymakers operate in a policymaking environment of which they have limited knowledge and even less control. There is no all-powerful 'centre' making policy from the 'top down'. We need to incorporate this environment into policy analysis: these factors warn us against 'single-shot' policy analysis in which there is a one-size-fits-all solution, and the idea that the selection of a policy solution from the 'top' sets in motion an inevitable cycle of legitimation, implementation, and evaluation. A simple description of a problem and its solution may be attractive, but success may also depend on persuading your audience at 'the centre' about the need to: (a) learn continuously and adapt their strategies through processes such as trial and error and (b) cooperate with many other 'centres' to address problems that no single actor can solve.

What Do Policy Analysts Need to Learn About the Politics of Knowledge?

It is more difficult to argue that more enlightenment about marginalisation, inequalities, and decolonisation will aid the pragmatic policy analyst. Yet, at the very least, discussions about widening the pool of policy-relevant knowledge (to make policy analysis better informed) and engaging with many actors and groups (to demonstrate consultation and aid stakeholder 'ownership') may not be such a hard sell. If so, a commitment to effective policy analysis may overlap *somewhat* with a commitment to equitable policy analysis practices, albeit with the potential for the latter to be reduced to window dressing. Further, for many, policy analyst skills, to frame policy problems and find politically feasible solutions, may be put to good use to 'change the world' *and* satisfy a client.

In such cases, the policy analyst will likely face a stark ethical dilemma about how to draw the line between an appropriate persuasive argument and inappropriate manipulation. However, the solution is not simply to withdraw from any form of psychology-informed communication. Policy research suggests that such a move will undermine the effectiveness of policy analysis. Rather, we need to incorporate ethical questions into policy analysis training, to develop a set of principles to guide our behaviour in these new circumstances. Policy analysis is already about critical thinking about a policy problem, which involves thinking about the role of the analyst and how not to cross ethical lines. Further, those lines shift according to levels of inequalities. Put simply, we should not pretend to be sticking to some notion of professional objectivity if it contributes to social and political marginalisation.

A Summary of Five-Step Approaches

One way to imagine this continuous overlap between these approaches is to revisit the five-step plan, considering three perspectives each time (Table 13.1). It suggests that:

Table 13.1 Three perspectives on five-step policy analysis methods

Policy analysis	*Policy process*	*Critical policy analysis*
Define a policy problem identified by your client	Incorporate a policymaker's willingness and ability to understand and solve the policy problem	Identify the extent to which your definition fits into current paradigms. Challenge dominant ways to frame issues
Identify technically and politically feasible solutions	Identify the mix of policy instruments already being used, and why. For example, is a new instrument feasible because it builds on others?	Encourage inclusive ways to generate knowledge and multiple perspectives to inform the definition of, and solution, to problems
Use value-based criteria and political goals to compare solutions	Identify the ways in which actors cooperate or compete to define and rank values	Consider ways to co-produce the rules of solution production and evaluation
Predict the outcome of each feasible solution	Consider the existing mix of policies and the potentially disproportionate effect of your recommendation	Focus on the disproportionate impact on marginalised groups, such as via gender and race budgeting analysis
Make a recommendation to your client	Recommendations on policy choices are incomplete without recommendations on how to adapt to policymaking systems. For example, in the absence of centralisation, how can you deliver this instrument?	Co-produce your recommendations with stakeholders, to make sure that you anticipate and respect their reaction to your proposals

Source: author's own

1. *Problem definition* is about identifying your client's understanding, and ability to understand and solve the problem, and your duty to challenge dominant ways of thinking.
2. *Identifying solutions* is about technical and political feasibility, the current mix of instruments, and the ways in which you co-produce research to inform solutions.
3. *Comparing solutions* is about using value-based criteria and political goals, a competition or cooperative effort to attach value to outcomes, and effective rules to foster cooperation.
4. *Predicting outcomes* is about technical prediction and identifying trade-offs, anticipating the non-linear impact of new solutions, and identifying the disproportionate impact on marginalised groups.
5. *Making a recommendation* is about incorporating policy goals, the limitations provided by policymaking systems, and the need to co-produce recommendations with a wide range of groups.

Overall, this book focuses on the problems with divorcing (a) the scientific analysis of policy problems from (b) scientific studies of policymaking, which help identify the limits to policy analysis and action, and (c) the politics of choices, to determine whose knowledge counts as policy-relevant knowledge, and whose interests determine the final outcome. Empirically, it shows that policy analysis will be of limited value unless we incorporate policymaker psychology and policymaking complexity into policy analysis. Normatively, it shows what policy analysis looks like when we move from a sole focus on the technocratic idea of 'evidence-based policymaking' towards equally persuasive forms of engagement, such as summed up in terms such as consensus seeking and co-production.

Reference

Stone, D. (2012). *Policy Paradox: The Art of Political Decision Making* (3rd ed.). London: Norton.

Annex: What Do We Want Public Policy Scholars to Learn?

Introduction

Learning about public policy requires us to focus on *what* to learn and *how* to learn. Phrases such as 'learning how to learn' (in education) and 'intelligent' or 'adaptive' policymaking (in policy analysis) are not so different. They both involve developing greater knowledge of public policy by developing analytical skills that can be used to understand and use knowledge in theory and practice. Such learning can relate to:

1. The 'basic science' of public policy. We focus on using policy models, concepts, theories, and frameworks to understand policymaking dynamics, from the actions of individual policymakers to the overall patterns of policymaking in complex systems.
2. The 'applied science' of policy analysis, in which we apply our knowledge of the policy process to identify a policy problem and possible solutions.

Ideally, there would be a high overlap between scientific and practical policy analysis, but students often learn quickly that there is a gap between theory-driven studies of the policy process and more hands-on analysis of how people should act within that process to identify problems and solutions.

Therefore, one key aim of this book is to help readers—with various backgrounds and motivations to learn—study public policy with reference to the same foundational 'story'. I provide a narrative of policy and the policy process, to represent substantive knowledge of the discipline of public policy, and use it as a key reference point throughout this book, to help identify how readers can learn about, engage in, and then produce new knowledge of the policy process.

A reader can decide to learn about basic or applied science or to think about how to apply insights from both types of studies. These choices often *seem* stark, particularly when university modules and textbooks relate only to one focus. In some cases, this disconnect can be addressed by combining modules on policy process research, analysis, and research methods, in a full (1–4 year) programme. In shorter, more introductory, online or executive courses, we need to make more difficult choices about the skills and knowledge we can reasonably expect someone to learn and apply. Some readers will graduate with bachelor's or master's level degree, perhaps seeking to apply a core set of skills to pursue theoretically informed policy analysis, while some will return from public or professional service to revisit their knowledge and analytical skills.

From that basic starting point, we can produce a series of broad learning outcomes that combine knowledge of the subject with the skills we require to understand the subject:

1. *Knowledge of key definitions of policy and of the main components of the policy process.* Most introductions to policy focus on the problem of defining it, and the insights we generate while trying. They identify the role of policymaker psychology, the complexity of the policy environment in which they engage, and key intermediate concepts such as the networks connecting people and systems.
2. *How to understand the policy process using established concepts.* Basic science students require some knowledge of the ways in which public policy research describes the process; to learn key concepts and how they are applied in theories and models; and to learn how to 'zoom in' to focus on individuals, then 'zoom out' to consider institutions and networks, and zoom out further to analyse policymaking systems. Applied science students learn about how to engage at various 'stages' of the 'policy cycle'. Combined analysis highlights a tendency of modern theories to find limited value in the 'stages' approach and a search for useful alternatives.

3. *How to conduct research in public policy.* Basic science teaching may focus on research skills to produce new knowledge. Applied science may focus on skills to combine new knowledge with the analysis of existing publications.

What Does a Combination of Skills Look like?
Many see policy research as a source of knowledge and skills that they can use in and around politics and policy, such as in one level or type of government (e.g. the civil service), or organisation with some need to engage with public policy. If so, the most practical thing to learn is how to conduct theory-informed policy analysis, in which they develop (a) skills to identify and research policy problems and feasible solutions and (b) understand the policy process in which they engage.

This combination of topics helps us reject the description of policy analysis as a rational and technical exercise, through a series of steps, even

Table A1 Key topics and question in basic and applied policy sciences

	Basic science (policy process research)	*Key overlaps*	*Applied science (policy analysis)*
Substantive knowledge	What is the policy process? How can we identify and measure policy change?	What is policy? How should we study it?	What is the policy problem? What policy solutions are technically and politically feasible?
Conceptual and analytical skills	Theoretical analysis. Micro, macro, and meso levels of analytical abstraction Frameworks, theories, concepts, and models	Conceptual and empirical analysis How useful is the 'policy cycle' to (a) understand the policy process and (b) engage in the policy process?	Policy analysis Problem definition, formulation, implementation, monitoring, and evaluation
Research skills	Using research methods to produce new knowledge of the policy process	Combining research methods—quantitative and qualitative methods, modelling, social networks analysis, ethnography	Using research methods to generate knowledge of a policy problem and calculate the likely success of solutions

Source: Author's own

if it comes with a description of key qualifications, such as in relation to time pressures, political constraints, and the need to treat clients as the main audience. These constraints tend to relate to the ability to complete your own work, rather than the constraints in policymaking systems that, to all intents and purposes, place severe limits on the ways in which anyone will seek to understand problems, and the technical and political feasibility of any solution.

A wider understanding of policy processes requires us to produce policy analyses and reflect on why people write them the way they do. The main advantage of this reflection, compared to texts that only focus on the nuts and bolts of analysis, is that it does not produce a cohort of students that present recommendations untethered from reality and unable to explain or anticipate what goes wrong *until they actually engage in politics in the real world*. The aim is not to give up, or only present modest policy analyses. Rather, it is to encourage students to engage in ambitious policy analysis with their eyes open.

Encouraging 'Intelligent Policymaking'
In coursework, we can combine exercises to develop specific skills then consider how those skills contribute to an overall approach to 'intelligent policymaking' (Sanderson 2009). Although difficult to pin down and define, intelligent or critical thinking is crucial to policy analysis. The world is too unpredictable, and it changes too much, for us to develop and stick to a specific type of analysis (such as cost-benefit analysis) and hope that it applies to all eventualities. Instead, Cairney and Weible (2017: 7) emphasise the development—in ourselves and, hopefully, in our audience—of critical thought and analysis:

> Scholars can help actors in the policy process to ask better questions, identify their own assumptions and cognitive filters and biases, see the world through different viewpoints, recognize the strengths and limitations of their information searches and networks, and better specify the source of their successes and failures. Above all else, we can dispense with the idea of comparing real-world policymaking with the myth of comprehensively rational action, to advise people not to give up their bounded and irrational minds but to look for opportunities to learn and adapt their strategies to better achieve their goals. To make it happen, we need to recognize the combined value of basic and applied science.

One step to combining policy analysis and policy process research is to modify the former according to the insights of the latter. In other words, consider how a 'new policy sciences' inspired policy analysis differs from the analyses already provided by five-step guides.

It could turn out that the effects of our new insights on a policy briefing could be so subtle that you might blink and miss them. Or, there are so many possibilities from which to choose that it is impossible to provide a blueprint for new policy science advice. Therefore, I encourage students to be creative in their policy analysis and reflective in their assessment of their analysis. Our aim is to think about the skills you need to analyse policy, from producing or synthesising evidence, to crafting an argument based on knowing your audience, and considering how your strategy might shift in line with a shifting context.

To aid creativity, I set a range of tasks so that students can express themselves in different ways, to different audiences, with different constraints. For example, we can learn how to be punchy and concise from a three-minute presentation or 500-word blog, and use that skill to get to the point more quickly in policy analysis or clarify the research question in the essay. The overall effect should be that students can take what they have learned from each exercise and use it for the others. In each section below, I reproduce the ways in which I describe this mix of coursework to students then, in each box, note the underlying rationale.

1. A three-minute spoken presentation to your peers in a seminar

In three minutes, you need to identify a problem, describe one or more possible solutions, and end your presentation in a convincing way. For example, if you don't make a firm recommendation, what can you say to avoid looking like you are copping out? Focus on being persuasive, to capture your audience's imagination. Focus on the policy context, in which you want to present a problem as solvable (who will pay attention to an intractable problem?) but not make inflated claims about how one action can solve a major problem. Focus on providing a memorable take-home message.

The presentation can be as creative as you wish, but it should not rely on PowerPoint in the room. Imagine that none of the screens works or that you are making your pitch to a policymaker as you walk along the street: can you make this presentation engaging and memorable without any reference to someone else's technology? Can you do it without just reading out your notes? Can you do it well in *under* three minutes? We will then devote five minutes to questions from the audience about your presentation. Being an active part of the audience—and providing peer review—is as important as doing a good presentation of your own.

> **Box A1 Rationale for Three-Minute Presentation**
> If students perform this task first (before the coursework is due), it gives them an initial opportunity to see how to present only the most relevant information, and to gauge how an audience responds to their ideas. Audience questions provide further peer-driven feedback. I also plan a long seminar to allow each student (in a group of 15–20 people) to present, then ask all students about which presentation they remember and why. This exercise helps students see that they are competing with each other for limited policymaker attention, and learn from their peers about what makes an effective pitch. Maybe you are wondering why I discourage PowerPoint. It's largely because it will cause each presenter to go way over time by cramming in too much information, and this problem outweighs the benefit of being able to present an impressive visualisation. I prefer to encourage students to only tell the audience what they will remember (by only presenting what *they* remember).

2. A policy analysis paper, and 3. A reflection on your analysis

Provide a policy analysis paper which has to make a substantive argument or recommendation in approximately two pages (1000 words), on the assumption that busy policymakers won't read much else before deciding whether or not to pay attention to the problem and your solutions. Then provide a reflection paper (also approximately 1000 words) to reflect your theoretical understanding of the policy process. You can choose how to split the 2000 word length, between analysis and reflection. You can give each exercise 1000 each (roughly a two-page analysis), provide a shorter analysis and more reflection, or widen the analysis and reject the need for conceptual reflection. The choice is yours to make, as long as you justify your choice in your reflection.

When writing policy analysis, I ask you to keep it super-short on the assumption that you have to make your case quickly to people with 99 other things to do. For example, what can you tell someone in one paragraph or a half-page to get them to read all two pages? It is tempting to try to tell someone everything you know, because everything is connected and to simplify is to describe a problem simplistically. Instead, be smart enough to know that such self-indulgence won't impress your audience. In person, they might smile politely, but their eyes are looking at the elevator lights. In writing, they can skim your analysis or simply move on. So, use these three statements to help you focus less on your need to supply information and more on their demand:

1. *Your aim is not to give a full account of a problem.* It is to get powerful people to care about it.
2. *Your aim is not to give a painstaking account of all possible solutions.* It is to give a sense that at least one solution is feasible and worth pursuing.
3. *Your guiding statement should be*: policymakers will only pay attention to your problem if they think they can solve it, and without that solution being too costly.

Otherwise, I don't like to give you too much advice because I want you to be creative about your presentation; to be confident enough to take chances and feel that you'll see the reward of making a leap. At the very least, you have three key choices to make about how far you'll go to make a point:

1. *Who is your audience?* Our discussion of the limits to centralised policymaking suggest that your most influential audience will not necessarily be an elected policymaker, but who else would it be?
2. *How 'manipulative' should you be?* Our discussions of 'bounded rationality' and 'evidence-based policymaking' suggest that policymakers combine 'rational' and 'irrational' shortcuts to gather information and make choices. So, do you appeal to their desire to set goals and gather a lot of scientific information, make an emotional appeal, or rely on Riker-style heresthetics?
3. *What is your role?* Contemporary discussions of science advice to government highlight unresolved debates about the role of unelected advisors: should you simply lay out some possible solutions or advocate one solution strongly?

For our purposes, there are no wrong answers to these questions. Instead, I want you to make and defend your decisions. That is the aim of your policy paper 'reflection': to 'show your work'. You still have some room to be creative in your reflection: tell me what you know about policy theory and how it informed your decisions. Here are some examples, but it is up to you to decide what to highlight:

1. Show how your understanding of policymaker psychology helped you decide how to present information on problems and solutions.
2. Extract insights from policy theories, such as from punctuated equilibrium theory on policymaker attention, multiple streams analysis on timing and feasibility, or the narrative policy framework (NPF) on how to tell persuasive stories.
3. Explore the implications of the lack of 'comprehensive rationality' and absence of a 'policy cycle': feasibility is partly about identifying the extent to which a solution is 'doable' when central governments have limited powers. What 'policy style' or policy instruments would be appropriate for the solution you favour?

I use the following questions to guide the marking on the policy paper: Tailored properly to a clearly defined audience? Punchy and concise summary? Clearly defined problem? Good evidence or argument behind the solution? Clear recommendations backed by a sense that the solution is feasible? Evidence of substantial reading, accompanied by well-explained further reading?

In my experience of marking, successful students gave a very clear and detailed account of the nature and size of the policy problem. The best reports used graphics and/or statistics to describe the problem in several ways. Some identified a multi-faceted problem—such as in health outcomes, and health inequalities—without presenting confusing analysis. Some were able to present an image of urgency, to separate this problem from the many others that might grab policymaker attention. Successful students presented one or more solutions which seemed technically and/or politically feasible. By technically feasible, I mean that there is a good chance that the policy will work as intended if implemented. For example, they provided evidence of its success in a comparable country (or in the past) or outlined models designed to predict the effects of specific policy instruments. By politically feasible, I mean that you consider how open your audience would be to the solution, and how likely the suggestion is to be acceptable to key policymakers. Some students added to a good discussion of feasibility by comparing the pros/cons of different scenarios. In contrast, some relatively weak reports proposed solutions which were vague, untested, and/or not likely to be acted upon.

> **Box A2 Rationale for Policy Analysis and Reflection**
> Students already have five-step policy analysis texts at their disposal, and they give some solid advice about the task. However, I want to encourage students to think more about how their knowledge of the policy process will guide their analysis. *First, what do you do if you think that one audience will buy your argument, and another reject it wholeheartedly?* Just pretend to be an objective analyst and put the real world in the 'too hard' pile? Or, do you recognise that policy analysts are political actors and make your choices accordingly? For me, an appeal to objectivity combined with insufficient recognition of the ways in which people respond emotionally to information is a total cop-out. I don't want to contribute to a generation of policy analysts who provide long, rigorous, and meticulous reports that few people read and fewer people use. Instead, I want students to show me how to tell a convincing story with a clear moral, or frame policy analysis to grab their audience's attention and generate enthusiasm to try to solve a problem. Then, I want them to reflect on how *they* draw the line between righteous persuasion and unethical manipulation.
>
> *Second, how do you account for policymaking complexity?* You can't assume that there is a cycle in which a policymaker selects a solution and it sets in train a series of stages towards successful implementation. Instead, you need to think about the delivery of your policy as much as the substance. Students have several choices. In some cases, they will describe how to deliver policy in a multi-level or multi-centric environment, in which, say, a central government actor will need to use persuasion or cooperation rather than command-and-control. Or, if they are feeling energetic, they might compare a top-down delivery option with support for Ostrom-style polycentric arrangements. Maybe they'll recommend pilots and/or trial and error, to monitor progress continuously instead of describing a one-shot solution. Maybe they'll reflect on multiple streams analysis and think about how you can give dependable advice in a policy process containing some serendipity. Who knows? Policy process research is large and heterogeneous, which opens the possibility for some creative solutions that I won't be able to anticipate in advance.

4. One kind of blog post (for the policy analysis).

Write a short and punchy blog post which recognises the need to make an argument succinctly and grab attention with the title and first sentence/paragraph, on the assumption that your audience will be reading it on their phone and will move on to something else quickly. In this exercise, your blog post is connected to your policy analysis. Think, for example, about how you would make the same case for a policy solution to a wider 'lay' audience. Or, use the blog post to gauge the extent to which your client could sell your policy solution. If they would struggle, should you make this recommendation in the first place?

Your blog post audience is wider than your policy analysis audience. You are trying to make an argument that will capture the attention of a larger group of people who are interested in politics and policy, but without being specialists. They will likely access your post from Twitter/Facebook or via a search engine. This constraint produces a new requirement, to: present a punchy title which sums up the whole argument in under 280 characters (a statement is often better than a vague question); summarise the whole argument in approximately 100 words in the first paragraph (what is the problem and solution?); then, provide more information up to a maximum of 500 words. The reader can then be invited to read the whole policy analysis.

The style of blog posts varies markedly, so you should consult many examples before attempting your own (e.g. compare the London School of Economics (LSE) with The Conversation and newspaper blogs to get a sense of variations in style). When you read other posts, take note of their strengths and weaknesses. For example, many posts associated with newspapers introduce a personal or case study element to ground the discussion in an emotional appeal. Sometimes this works, but sometimes it causes the reader to scroll down quickly to find the main argument. Perhaps ironically, I recommend storytelling but I often skim past people's stories. Many academic posts are too long (well beyond your 500 limit), take too long to get to the point, and do not make explicit recommendations, so you should not emulate them. You should aim to be better than the scholars whose longer work you read. You should not just chop down your policy analysis to 500 words; you need a new kind of communication.

Hopefully, by the end of this fourth task, you will appreciate the transferable life skills. I have generated some uncertainty about your task to reflect the sense among many actors that they don't really know how to make a persuasive case and who to make it to. We can follow some basic Bardach-style guidance, but a lot of this kind of work relies on trial-and-error. I maintain a short word count to encourage you to get to the point, and I bang on about 'stories' in modules to encourage you to present a short and persuasive story to policymakers.

This process seems weird at first, but isn't it also intuitive? For example, next time you're in my seminar, measure how long it takes you to get bored and look forward to the weekend. Then imagine that policymakers have the same attention span as you. That's how long you have to make your case! Policymakers are not magical beings with an infinite attention span. In fact, they are busier and under more pressure than us, so you need to make your pitch count.

> **Box A3 Rationale for Blog Post 1**
> This exercise forces students to make their case in 500 words. It helps them understand the need to communicate in different ways to different audiences. It suggests that successful communication is largely about knowing how your audience consumes information, rather than telling people all you know. I gauge success according to questions such as: Punchy and eye-grabbing title? Tailored to an intelligent 'lay' audience rather than a specific expert group? Clearly defined problem? Good evidence or argument behind the solution? Clear recommendations backed by a sense that the solution is feasible? Well-embedded weblinks to further relevant reading?

5. Writing a theory-informed essay

I tend to set this simple-looking question for coursework in policy modules: *what is policy, how much has it changed, and why?* Students get to choose the policy issue, timeframe, political system, and relevant explanatory concepts.

On the face of it, it looks very straightforward. Give it a few more seconds, and you can see the difficulties:

1. We spend a lot of time in class agreeing that it seems almost impossible to define policy.
2. There are many possible measures of policy change.

3. There is an almost unmanageable number of models, concepts, and theories to use to explain policy dynamics.

I try to encourage some creativity when solving this problem, but also advise students to keep their discussion as simple and jargon-free as possible (often by stretching an analogy with competitive diving, in which a well-executed simple essay can score higher than a belly-flopped hard essay).

Choosing a Format: The Initial Advice

1. Choose a policy area (such as health) or issue (such as alcohol policy).
2. Describe the nature of policy, and the extent of policy change, in a particular time period (such as in a particular era, after an event or constitutional change, or after a change in government).
3. Select one or more policy concepts or theory to help structure your discussion and help explain how and why policy has changed.

For example, a question might be: *What is tobacco policy in the UK, how much has it changed since the 1980s, and why?* I use this example because I try to answer that question myself, even though some of my work is too theory-packed to be a good model for a student essay (Cairney 2007 is essentially a bad model for students).

Choosing a Format: The Cautionary Advice
You may be surprised about how difficult it is to answer a simple question like 'what is policy?' and I will give you a lot of credit for considering how to define and measure it; by identifying, for example, the use of legislation/regulation, funding, staff, and 'nodality' (Hood and Margetts 2007) and/or by considering the difference between, say, policy as a statement of intent or a long-term outcome. In turn, a good description and explanation of policy change are difficult. If you are feeling ambitious, you can go further, to compare, say, two issues (such as tobacco and alcohol) or places (such as UK government policy and the policy of another country), but sometimes a simple and narrow discussion can be more effective. Similarly, you can use many theories or concepts to aid explanation, but one theory may do. Note that (a) your description of your research question, and your essay structure, is more important than (b) your decision on what topic or concepts to use.

Box A4 Rationale for the Essay
The wider aim is to encourage students to think about the relationship between different perspectives on policy theory and analysis. For example, in a blog and policy analysis paper they try to generate attention to a policy problem and advocate a solution. Then, they draw on policy theories and concepts to reflect on their papers, highlighting (say): the need to identify the most important audience; the importance of framing issues with a mixture of evidence and emotional appeals; and, the need to present 'feasible' solutions.

The reflection can provide a useful segue to the essay, since we're already identifying important policy problems, advocating change, reflecting on how best to encourage it—such as by presenting modest objectives—and then, in the essay, trying to explain (say) why governments have not taken that advice in the past. Their interest in the policy issue can prompt interest in researching the issue further; their knowledge of the issue and the policy process can help them develop politically aware policy analysis. All going well, it produces a virtuous circle.

Box A5 Rationale for Blog Post 2
I get students to do the analysis/reflection/blog combination in the first module, and an essay/blog combo in the second module. The second blog post has a different aim. Students use the 500 words to present a jargon-free analysis of policy change. The post represents a useful exercise in theory translation. Without it, students tend to describe a large amount of jargon because I am the audience and I understand it. By explaining the same thing to a lay audience, they are obliged to explain key developments in a plain language. This requirement should also help them present a clearer essay, because people (academics and students) often use jargon to cover the fact that they don't really know what they are saying.

REFERENCES

Cairney, P. (2007). A "Multiple Lenses" Approach to Policy Change: the Case of Tobacco Policy in the UK. *British Politics, 2*(1), 45–68.

Cairney, P., & Weible, C. (2017). The New Policy Sciences: Combining the Cognitive Science of Choice, Multiple Theories of Context, and Basic and Applied Analysis. *Policy Sciences, 50*(4), 619–627.

Hood, C., & Margetts, H. (2007). *The Tools of Government in the Digital Age.* London: Red Globe Press.

Sanderson, I. (2009). Intelligent Policy Making for a Complex World: Pragmatism, Evidence and Learning'. *Political Studies, 57*(4), 699–719.

INDEX

A

Actors, vi, 4, 7, 12, 17, 19, 24, 34–36, 41–44, 51–54, 56, 59–61, 63, 65, 72–77, 79, 84, 86–88, 93, 101–105, 118, 123–127, 131–133, 140–144, 149, 156, 161, 162

Ambiguity, 44, 59, 75, 79, 92, 103, 118, 119

Argumentation, 17, 41, 120

Art and craft, 36, 37, 88, 91, 120

B

Be concise (communicate clearly), 16

Beliefs, 13, 14, 16, 18, 28, 45, 50–54, 56, 57, 59, 61, 62, 64, 73, 88, 103, 124, 125, 140, 142–145, 148

Bounded rationality, 7, 50, 60, 61, 76, 102, 117, 148, 159

C

Centre (and central control, 'core executive'), 7, 34, 35, 50, 52, 64, 102, 127, 141, 149

Clients, v, vi, 4, 6, 11–18, 23, 24, 33–37, 39–41, 53, 72, 88, 92, 94, 102–104, 113, 118–120, 129, 140, 141, 148, 149, 151, 156, 162

Coalitions, 51, 53, 54, 57, 61–63, 124, 125, 143

Cognitive bias, 50, 56

Complexity (and complex systems), 4, 5, 7, 34, 40, 41, 44, 51, 53–65, 92, 101, 102, 106, 130–134, 149, 151, 153, 154, 161

Context, vi, 3, 4, 6, 8, 18, 19, 25, 29, 30, 37–40, 45, 50, 53–65, 73–75, 77–80, 85–89, 92, 93, 101–103, 105, 111, 117, 118, 120, 124, 132, 135, 140, 142, 143, 157

168 INDEX

Co-production, 5, 81–83, 86, 111–113, 151
Cost-benefit analysis (CBA), 3, 5, 21, 37, 42, 43, 50, 81, 86, 94, 120, 156
Cost-effectiveness analysis (CEA), 21
Critical policy analysis, vi, vii, 79

D
Decolonisation (and colonisation), v, vi, 71, 79–81, 83, 88, 120, 149
Design thinking, 19, 95

E
Efficiency, 12–15, 19–21, 37, 74
Emotions, 29, 50, 52, 53, 73, 103, 144
Empathy, 19
Enlightenment, 13, 79, 140, 149
Equity (fairness), 14, 19, 20, 93
Ethics, 8, 22, 26–29, 40, 41, 43, 80, 81, 93–94, 119, 142–145, 149, 150
Evaluation, 4, 13, 18, 19, 22, 23, 25, 42, 43, 58, 65, 101, 102, 149
Events, 11, 27, 50, 56, 62, 126, 142, 164
Evidence, 12, 15, 16, 19, 22–23, 30, 38, 41, 43–45, 52, 53, 58, 59, 62–64, 75, 77, 79, 80, 84–86, 94, 103, 110–113, 119, 124–126, 133, 140–145, 157, 160, 163, 165
Evidence-based policymaking, 37, 109–111, 134, 135, 159
Experience, vi, 18, 22, 43, 74, 81–83, 86, 140, 160

F
Fairness, *see* Equity
Feasible (and feasibility), 3, 4, 12, 13, 15, 16, 18–20, 42–44, 53, 54, 59, 64, 74, 88, 93, 104, 105, 118, 119, 124–127, 140, 143, 149, 151, 155, 156, 159–161, 163, 165
Feminism, v, 71
5-step policy analysis, vii, 6, 37, 50, 73, 94, 95, 102, 104, 148, 150, 161
Framing, 25, 28, 51, 52, 60, 65, 74, 76, 81, 93, 103, 104, 142, 144, 148, 165
See also Problem definition
Freedom, 12, 19, 74, 94, 131
Functional requirements (versus policymaking reality), 7, 102

G
Governance, 64, 111, 112

H
Heuristics, 6, 29, 42, 51, 100, 101, 117, 141, 143
Hierarchy of evidence, 110, 111
Human dignity (and human rights, flourishing), vii, 4, 8, 15, 20, 84, 89, 92

I
Ideas, v, 3, 4, 8, 19, 21, 26, 30, 35, 37, 38, 40, 42, 43, 50, 51, 54, 62, 65, 72, 78, 79, 82–84, 86, 88, 91, 92, 101, 110, 112, 124, 127, 129, 133, 134, 142, 144, 149, 151, 156, 158

Impact, v, vi, 4, 6, 8, 11, 14, 15, 18–22, 26, 35, 43, 44, 50, 52, 54, 57, 58, 61, 64, 74, 79, 81, 83, 86, 93, 102, 105, 106, 118, 119, 125–127, 133, 134, 139–145, 147, 148, 151
Inequalities, vi, vii, 8, 58, 72, 74, 80, 83–84, 87, 89, 110, 127, 141, 147, 149, 150, 160
Institutional Analysis and Development framework (IAD), 63–64, 132
Institutions, 18, 20, 52, 54, 58, 60, 63, 75, 78, 83, 87, 88, 117, 132, 142, 154

J
Judgement, 12, 19–21, 24, 38, 51, 57, 58, 141

K
Knowledge, vi, vii, 4–7, 16, 18, 22–24, 26, 30, 37, 38, 40, 41, 43–45, 52, 65, 71–89, 91–93, 95, 102, 103, 109–113, 118–121, 123, 134, 143, 147, 149–151, 153–155, 161, 165
See also Synthesis; Whose knowledge counts?

L
Lasswell, H. D., 4, 99, 101
Learning, 40, 42, 43, 52, 62, 64, 100, 110, 111, 131, 132, 153, 154

M
Manipulation, 28, 29, 51, 76–77, 88, 149, 161
Marginalisation (and marginalised), vi, 58, 80–82, 86–87, 89, 120, 121, 141, 147, 149–151
Methods, 3–5, 13, 17, 19, 21–22, 24–26, 29, 36–39, 42–44, 50, 73, 80, 82, 84, 85, 87, 92, 94, 103, 110–112, 119–121, 134, 150, 154
Morals, 22, 41, 53, 57, 73, 81, 148, 161
Multi-centric policymaking, 34, 117
Multiple streams analysis, 58–59, 125, 160, 161

N
Narrative/stories, vii, 17, 24, 25, 29, 30, 33–39, 49, 51, 53, 56–57, 60, 72–77, 81, 87, 88, 92, 93, 100, 103, 105, 110–113, 125, 127, 130–135, 140, 142, 143, 145, 148, 154, 161–163
Need, 6, 7, 12, 15, 17–19, 24, 33, 71–89, 92, 93, 95, 99–106, 118, 124, 125, 130, 132, 134, 135, 140, 142, 148–151, 154–159, 161–163, 165
Networks, 35, 36, 41, 43, 44, 53, 54, 60, 64, 65, 124, 125, 127, 142, 154, 156
New policy sciences, 157
Normative, 13, 19, 22, 40, 93–94, 103, 106, 111, 117, 118

P

Paradigm, 56, 84, 142
Policy analysis as a profession, 38, 42
Policy cycle, 7, 23, 37, 44, 49, 50, 53, 55, 58, 59, 65, 92, 95, 100–102, 154, 160, 161
Policy design, 38, 41, 42, 57–58, 87, 110, 111
  See also Social construction and policy design
Policy entrepreneur, 7, 123–127
Policymaking environments, 6–8, 33, 34, 44, 54, 93, 102, 125, 126, 143, 148, 149
Policy paradox, 72–77, 148
Policy solutions (or options, alternatives), 4, 12–16, 18, 20–22, 36, 44, 57, 64, 92, 94, 100, 105, 148
Power, v, vi, 5, 6, 8, 16–18, 22, 43, 50, 51, 58, 60, 65, 71–89, 103, 118, 120, 123, 127, 134, 141, 143–144, 147, 160
Pragmatism, 4, 22, 36, 40, 88, 141, 148
Prediction, 12, 13, 15, 19, 22, 23, 105, 151
Problem definition, 14, 16–18, 41, 72, 77, 78, 81, 93, 94, 102, 103, 118, 151
  See also Framing
Psychology, v, 5, 19, 50–53, 103, 141, 148, 149, 151, 154, 160
Punctuated equilibrium, 59–61, 160

R

Race/racism, vi, 71, 72, 83, 87, 88, 94, 120
Randomised control trials (RCTs), 27, 110, 112
Rational policy analysis, 34
Recommendations, v, vii, 6, 12, 13, 15, 21, 34, 50, 65, 95, 101, 104, 119, 140, 151, 156–158, 160, 162, 163
Respect, 81, 85, 93, 110, 120, 141
Risk, 26–29, 74, 76, 120, 125, 129, 131
Role as a policy analyst, 7, 113, 117–121

S

Security, 13, 74, 77, 87, 131
Skills (of policy analysts), 4, 36, 125, 126, 149, 153–155, 157
Social construction and policy design, 57–58, 144
Social justice, 83, 84, 87
Speak truth to power, 89, 141
Stages, *see* Policy cycle
Stakeholder, 13, 14, 16, 17, 21, 40–43, 81, 82, 86, 93, 104, 106, 110, 112, 113, 140, 149
Statistics, 27, 28, 43, 79, 92, 160
Status quo, 18, 24, 44, 51, 72, 82, 88, 103, 141
Styles of policy analysis, 4, 40
Sustainability, 20, 134
Synthesis (of evidence or knowledge), 85, 157
Systems thinking, 8, 106, 129–135

T

Trade-offs, 12–15, 19, 41, 44, 51, 94, 112, 142, 151

U

Uncertainty, 26–27, 29, 41, 42, 44, 59, 61, 79, 92, 94, 103, 118–120, 140, 162

V

Values, 12, 13, 15, 16, 18–22, 26, 36, 39, 42, 44, 45, 49–51, 53, 56–58, 73, 74, 76, 77, 80, 81, 85, 88, 92–94, 99, 104, 110, 111, 118, 119, 125, 132, 144, 145, 148, 151, 154, 156

W

What's the problem represented to be?' (WRP), 77–79

Whose knowledge counts?, 110

GPSR Compliance

The European Union's (EU) General Product Safety Regulation (GPSR) is a set of rules that requires consumer products to be safe and our obligations to ensure this.

If you have any concerns about our products, you can contact us on

ProductSafety@springernature.com

In case Publisher is established outside the EU, the EU authorized representative is:

Springer Nature Customer Service Center GmbH
Europaplatz 3
69115 Heidelberg, Germany

www.ingramcontent.com/pod-product-compliance
Lightning Source LLC
LaVergne TN
LVHW020426070526
838199LV00004B/293

9 783030 661212